RUN
FROM THE SHADOW

A NOVEL BY
JAMES MCJUNKIN

To Abigail and Samuel … *you know who you are.*
Your faith, your courage, and your perseverance, has inspired many….

And to the 63 million refugees currently displaced by the threat of persecution and violence all around the world.

Contents

Preface 4
Prologue 7
Chapter
  1   Nigerian Strife 10
  2   Wrong Number 23
  3   Test of Tolerance 30
  4   Flight from Fear 45
  5   A New Beginning 55
  6   A Rough Start 65
  7   The Last Straw 78
  8   Costa Rica 87
  9   Nicaragua 99
  10 Caught in the Net 110
  11 Centro de Albergue de Migrantes 121
  12 Honduras to Guatemala 133
  13 Grueling Passage 143
  14 Rio Suchiate to Mexico 155
  15 Tales of Terror 164
  16 Race to the Border 175
  17 Welcome to America 187
  18 Abigail's Angels 194
  19 Finishing Strong 207
Epilogue 217
Map of the Journey 231
Photo Gallery 233
Acknowledgements 243
References 244

Preface

I did not intend to write *this* book.

For several years, I had contemplated the writing of a fiction novel. I had imagined that the book would be of the spy thriller genre'— my version of a "Jason Bourne" style action/adventure, since I am quite fond of such writing. All that I needed was a compelling core idea, a clever plot, engaging characters, and the selection of appropriate time period and location … It was as good as done! I had, certainly, never considered writing a true story, based on the lives of an obscure African couple.

In early 2016, I had the opportunity to meet this amazing couple, and begin to learn of their compelling story. I encountered these special individuals and their two children, on a typical Sunday morning following the close of the morning's worship service. Throughout the service, I had heard disturbing raspy gasps of an infant who seemed to be struggling for breath. After the service, I spotted the new guests with their two little boys, a 3 year old, and a newborn. I approached to introduce myself and welcome them to our church, quickly discovering that they were refugees from Africa, and were here in San Diego only temporarily, planning to continue their journey to Canada. They would be staying here while their two week old son was being treated for a life threatening respiratory condition. I wished them well as they left and did not expect to see them again.

Several days later, I was requested to visit a local children's hospital in order to pray with the couple, for the baby, who had just been admitted for surgery. The infant had been born with a constricted trachea, causing him great distress with both breathing and feeding. As we sat around a table in the hospital courtyard that day, talking and praying together, I began to learn of the family's incredible journey — a journey **from death to life**.

This is not a story about "religion" or other "churchy" things, but it is a story of *faith* — the remarkable personal faith of two amazing people who persevered over a remarkably grueling and dangerous one year journey, traveled by airplane, bus, raft, horseback, and on foot, and spanning three continents, fourteen countries, and covering over 17,000 miles, is an undeniable testament of God's *faithfulness* to those who trust in him.

In addition to relating the important factual events of the story, I have introduced additional events, plausible circumstances, and fictional characters, in order to relate the story in a more cohesive form.

The couple's real names have not been used, at their request.

A great many lives were impacted, during the course of the family's stay in San Diego, as people had the opportunity to hear their story and witness their incredible faith, first hand.

I am confident that they will continue to have even greater impact in their new country and to be used by God in ways that none of us can imagine!

Webster defines the word *inspire* as being derived from the Latin word, *"inspirare," to blow upon or into, as by divine or supernatural influence.* This was an occasion when God blessed me to hear an amazing, faith building life experience and, I believe, *inspired* me to write about it.

After hearing their story, I just felt that I must share it.

May the reader draw encouragement, inspiration, and increased faith, from their story as well.

Prologue

It was 10:30 p.m. Monica Sanchez was on her way to the hospital's employee break room, when her friend, Linda, stopped her in the third floor, Labor and Delivery, hallway. Monica, an experienced delivery nurse, loved her job, but she had already been on duty for 8 hours, and was more than ready to get off her feet.

"Monica, I really hate to ask you but I have a huge favor to ask. I absolutely must get home to relieve my kid's sitter. My husband called and said he would be late and I just have to let her go home! If you could fill in for me just for an hour, I will come back and work the rest of your shift for you.

"Sure Linda," Monica replied, "not too much happening on the floor right now anyway. Just one woman with severe labor pains, brought in by the police."

Monica could hear the sounds of moaning coming from room 312, well before she reached it. As she entered, a nurse's aide was leaving, having just helped the patient change into a hospital gown.

"Hello, my name is Monica I am the delivery nurse on duty tonight. I see that your name is Abigail. That's a beautiful name; like Abigail from the Bible!"

"You must be a Christian, Monica, since you know of the name. I am a Christian as well."

"And who is this little guy, your son?" Monica inquired, smiling.

"Yes, this is my little boy, Saul. He is 3 years old," she answered.

"Is there anything I can do to make you comfortable until the doctor examines you?" Monica asked.

"The doctor won't give me anything for the pain; he says it's dangerous for the baby. I would love to take a shower if I could. I haven't been allowed to take a shower for days!"

"Of course Abigail, I will get things ready for you and help you into the bathroom," Monica answered, wondering, "Where had Abigail come from, why the woman had not been allowed to bathe and why had she been brought here by the police?"

Abigail was back in bed, after showering both herself and her son, by the time Monica stopped by to check on her again.

"If it is not too personal, can you share with me why you and your son were brought here by the authorities?" Monica inquired.

"I was brought here from the Immigration detention center where we have been held for the past six days. They took my family to the jail after we requested asylum at the border. I don't even know where my husband is being held or if he is OK. He must be so worried about us!"

"Oh Abigail, that is horrible! Will you have to return to jail after the baby is delivered?"

"Yes," Abigail answered, now sobbing, "I'm sure the police will take us back after the baby is delivered and if the baby does not come now they will take us back to jail. We only wanted to get to my sister's house in Canada, so we could have a life!"

Monica, whose heart was touched and now genuinely concerned, asked, "Tell me more about where your family came from and why have you been put in jail?"

"Monica, do you really want to know? It is a long story of our journey. It began about one year ago in Angola."

"Yes Abigail, I would like to hear your story."

With that, Abi began to recount the unbelievable events of her family's long journey to freedom.

Chapter 1

Nigerian Strife

It was 2:55 p.m. when the blast ripped through the rear of Terminus market. Even though the bomb had been detonated some distance away, Samuel had been thrown to the ground and sat stunned but unhurt in the pile of tires, ripped umbrellas and transmission gears.

Samuel scrambled to his feet, still deaf from the concussion. He could see nothing but thick black smoke and fire as he looked back toward the direction of the blast. His thoughts jumped immediately to his father who had been expected any minute. Was he OK? Had he been caught in the blast? He should have been here by now. Samuel's heart raced.

The day had begun just like any other Saturday morning for the young Nigerian mechanic.

It was nearly 6 a.m. by the time that Samuel Okotie-Eboh backed his Gray Toyota 4Runner out of the small rutted dirt drive which served as both parking lot and outdoor shop extension for the father-son auto repair and conversion business. He had intended to depart earlier for the Terminus Market in central Jos but underestimated the time required to load so many boxes of heavy transmission gears and other assorted parts.

For two years now, Samuel 29, and Olawale, his 53-year-old father, had lived behind the shop, sharing a small two-bedroom apartment that had been added on following the unexpected death of his mother, and the sudden departure of his older sister to neighboring Chad. His three other siblings and their families had fled to Angola, one year earlier, out of fear of Boko Harem and their increasingly violent and frequent attacks on Nigerian Christians.

Samuel could remember the times as a young boy that he, a Christian, and his many Muslim friends would play together and share meals in each other's homes. That all seemed so long ago. His mother would surely not have understood.

He had never remembered feeling afraid as a boy but times had changed for the worse. U.S. tourism had declined since 2011 when the state department had warned its citizens against travel to the Niger Delta. In addition to the occasional bombings, larger cities were no longer safe after the sun was down. One might find himself robbed, carjacked, raped, or even kidnapped for ransom.

Just last month 276 Christian schoolgirls had been kidnapped from their school dormitory in Chibok by the Islamic terrorist group Boko Haram. As of now they still had not yet been found or recovered. The identification of one's faith was now becoming a qualifier of life or death. In Northern Nigeria, Christians numbered only around 1% but in the 16 Central and Western states the percentage increased to around 30%. Plateau state, where Samuel's home city Jos was located between Abuja, the capitol, and the twin cities of Gamboru and Ngala, stood out at 70%, and the remaining eight Southern states were almost entirely Christian.

Boko Haram had now announced their intent to kill every Christian or force their conversion to Islam, in a ruthless bloody campaign that was now in process of sweeping across Nigeria. That chilling declaration had placed Plateau state and Jos immediately in the monster's path.

Now, with just father and son remaining in Jos, the sale of the old family home and the subsequent move into the shop/apartment had seemed the practical thing to do. Samuel greatly missed the joyful family home and close relationships with his siblings, but the opportunity to share the apartment and continue working with his father, helped minimize the loss.

Samuel switched the headlamps on. He shifted the manual transmission into gear and released the clutch, getting a bit of unintended wheel spin in the soft dirt even with the ponderous load. Samuel grimaced; he had wanted to be as quiet as possible, as it was his father's only morning to sleep in. He hoped he hadn't startled Olawale…

Samuel had a nostalgic fondness for the truck. Even though the '96 model was several years older than most of the customer cars that he and his father worked on, the 4Runner was still strong and reliable and not bad looking despite the ever present blanket of reddish Jos dust.

Like the majority of vehicles in Nigeria, the truck was a *"tokunbo" vehicle,* as vehicles imported into the country as used cars were called. Fully 80% of all vehicles in Nigeria were of *tokunbo* origin, mostly Japanese, but recently even more being imported from Europe, including many luxury models.

Seven years prior, Samuel himself, had performed the conversion on this truck from Japanese right side to Nigeria's left side driver controls. Olawale, his father had supervised the job but insisted that his, then, 22-year-old son, do all of the hands on wrenching. It was a good test of the skills learned in the many hours of apprenticing his accomplished mechanic father.

The shop had specialized in such conversions for 15 years now and was recognized throughout the city of Jos as a trustworthy source for both driver side conversions, as well as upgrades from manual to automatic transmissions.

Samuel turned right, west, onto Bauchi Road quickly passing over the Bunga River bridge and the nearby Student Village Hostel complex serving students of nearby University of Jos. He could have taken either road south, A23 or A25, about the same time and distance, either way, from this morning's destination, the huge Terminus Market in central Jos. Today he chose A236 the Bukuru expressway. Travel distance was only about 10 miles (16 km) but even this early on a Saturday, traffic could be heavy as he neared the Terminus area. On a good day it could be a 30-45 minute trip time. In spite of the commute, Samuel found the time therapeutic and a nice break from the long hours working inside the shop or outside in the hot dirt driveway, using the rusty steel A-frame hoist to yank out a stubborn engine or heavy transmission.

Since Samuel had grown up in Jos, he was fully accustomed to daily conditions in this part of West Africa; inadequate water treatment, waste disposal and drainage, lack of water for good personal hygiene and unreliable electric power. He was grateful though that this area was not littered with the solid waste from households and sewage lagoons that was common in the peripheral shanty towns. In contrast, nearby Abuja even had many luxury villas, hotels, and mansions.

Today, like most other weekends, he and his father would join more than 200 other vendors to sell their discounted, new and used auto parts, at the crowded Terminus Market. Olawale would relieve him later in the day which would allow Samuel to have a few precious hours in the afternoon for himself. The two men had realized early on that profits from the weekend market efforts had become an important cash supplement to their frequently inconsistent repair business.

Jos's Terminus Market was not as large as some other similar Nigerian markets such as Ladipo Market in Lagos or the United Berger Market along Oshodi expressway. However, it provided a great benefit not only to buyers and sellers, but it was also an important revenue source for the local economy.[1] The majority of sellers, primarily young men known as "freelancers," vied for sales with the flood of customers who crowded the square beginning at 9 a.m. each morning.

Besides providing a vast array of spare auto parts, tires, wheels, etc., the market was typically full of auto mechanics and technicians eager to assist with on-site diagnosis, repair, or other general services of buses, automobiles and trucks.[2]

It was just starting to become light as Samuel turned down Tafawa Balewa Street approaching the market entrance just past the Terminus roundabout. Traffic was already heavy with vendor trucks and countless taxies competing for space. All, apparently headed for the same destination.

Jos's ubiquitous yellow taxi-vans, mostly un-air-conditioned Type T2 or T3 Microbus Volkswagens, carried, as many as, 14 sweaty passengers, four to a seat, excluding the driver and conductor whose job was to crouch bravely in the *open* sliding door and shout out the next stop. Organized chaos. More annoying were the motorcycle taxis which carried up to three people, often without helmets, and would dart between cars, without warning and seemingly, without concern that a vehicle like Samuel's fully loaded 4Runner could not stop or change direction quickly.

As he had done each Saturday for the past six years, Samuel had made the 47 minute trip successfully, and without damage to truck or cargo. Maneuvering with some difficulty past an awkwardly parked white Toyota Sienna van, Samuel turned down the narrow lane that led to their assigned space near the end of the second row. The stall number, R-22, was easy to remember due to the countless R-22 version Toyota truck engines, of the same designation that he had rebuilt. Being located so close to the entrance meant good exposure and assured abundant customer traffic.

Against the backdrop of the market square with its drab outer perimeter and spaghetti-like array of power lines, emerged an explosion of color as sellers erected large umbrellas for sun protection over their stalls. The festive atmosphere always brought a smile to Samuel's face. It was only May 20th but already the days seemed hotter than he remembered.

Samuel positioned his truck with the tailgate close to his steel display table and began the task of unloading the heavy stacks of transmission gears. As display items, these parts benefited from particularly strong eye appeal, due to the bright gleaming surface ring patterns, inherent in their machining process. That natural bling was like a lure attracting fish.

"*How you dey?*" (How are you doing today?). Samuel's friend, John (pronounced *Joan*), shouted from behind a six foot wall of slightly used tires.

John favored Pidkin-English but was also comfortable speaking common English, the official language of Plateau state. Of the 500+ languages spoken in Nigeria, John and Samuel often switched between English, Pidkin-English, Hausa, or Portuguese. At the market, Pidkin was especially useful.

Samuel responded "*I dey fine*" (I'm doing well). John appeared from behind a stack of P215/65 R15 tires, offering a bowl of puff-puffs.

"Thank you, gi mi John." Samuel had not stopped to have breakfast and the bowl of the light sweetened dough balls were an unexpected treat. He downed the last puff-puff as he finished sorting his gear sets by type of teeth, helical, the more common, or straight-cut, a noisier but stronger option.

John, now switching to English said "it's been so crazy this month with the bombings first in Abuja and then attacks in Gamboru and Ngala." "Boko Haram is out of control! The military has done nothing to stop this madness."

"I'm afraid it will be happening here at any time" answered Samuel.

"You're right, the military is completely useless!" said John.

Armed with AK-47s and RPGs, militants had attacked Gamboru and Ngala using two armored personnel carriers stolen from the Nigerian military along with motorcycles and pick-up trucks. The attack occurred in the night when some residents were still sleeping. The militants opened fire on the people at a busy market that was open at night when temperatures were cool. Having set homes ablaze, the militants gunned down residents who tried to escape from the fire, killing hundreds and injuring hundreds more. Survivors had fled to Cameroon state.[3]

The market was scheduled to open at 9 a.m. but was often late due to its casual (inefficient) management but this morning the gates swung open on time. The usual surge of early customers rushed in hoping to have first pick of select items or to find specific parts and quickly get back to their repairs. Many of these men seeking parts were mechanics themselves and were regular customers at the market.

The morning so far had been quite generous to Samuel, with more parts sales than normal and even a couple of client bookings for driver side conversions to be done next week. Olawale would be very pleased and Samuel was eager to share the good news with him when he arrived later in the afternoon.

It was long past noon and Samuel was feeling particularly hungry. Strolling food vendors with their rolling carts were abundant during market hours and provided a smorgasbord of tasty choices. Today he was in the mood for *suya*, so he must be on the lookout for Hannah, an attractive young food vendor who cooked and sold the most delicious *suya*. Always perfectly seasoned.

Samuel had observed that Hannah was friendly with all her customers but was especially flirtatious with him. She had made it obvious that she might like to date him, but he had never had the courage to ask her. Samuel was attractive himself but somewhat shy. He had had a few dating relationships over the years but never anything serious. Life and work demands left little time for such things and it was not easy to find extra money for entertainment. He knew that he eventually desired a wife and family of his own, but that would have to wait.

Perfect timing; Hannah, with the food cart behind her, was weaving her way down the row, carefully picking her way through the crowds of men who, as always, seemed unconcerned or oblivious to her desire to pass by.

"Hello Samuel. It's so good to see you!"

"You as well," said Samuel. "I've been looking forward to having some of your wonderful *suya*."

"I was hoping that you might be looking forward to seeing me, not just the *suya*," said Hannah, attempting a sad look.

"Well, I always enjoy you coming by as well," he replied.

Hannah removed the lid on a large ceramic kettle and began to dish out steaming skewers of aromatic spiced meat. Samuel was accustomed to the serving amount being considerably more generous than others received. She then topped the meat with a handful of sharp, raw chopped onions and wrapped it all in newspaper.

"That will be 300 naira *boipren* (boyfriend)". Samuel handed her the money and she playfully squeezed his hand as she accepted the bills. Hannah smiled her thanks and made her way on down the row, pausing to turn back briefly and shout, "You should call me sometime Samuel," before disappearing in the stream of traffic.

"*E turkey Samuel*" (she is a babe Samuel), came from behind the wall of tires. "She likes you."

"Maybe John. Cane your line" (mind your own business), Samuel replied chuckling to himself.

Samuel had long finished his delicious *suya* and was impatient to be relieved by his father for the remainder of the afternoon. Olawale was usually there by 2 or 2:30 p.m. but was late. Their routine was to change cars, so Olawale would drive home in the 4Runner loaded with the remaining unsold parts, while Samuel would drive his father's car from its parking spot outside the market gates.

The concussion from the blast threw Samuel to the ground leaving him stunned and disoriented amidst the rubble of shredded asphalt and transmission parts. He must have been unconscious for a brief time. He was aware of an intense ringing in his ears, but could not separate individual sounds from the cacophony of noise around him. People were bleeding, screaming, crying, and sirens wailed in the distance as emergency vehicles began to respond to the horror.

Samuel scrambled to his feet, still deaf from the concussion. He could make out nothing but thick black smoke and fire as he looked back toward the direction of the blast. His thoughts jumped immediately to his father who had been expected any minute. Was he OK? ... Had he been caught in the blast? He should have been here by now... Samuel's heart raced ...

Several agonizing minutes had passed when Samuel finally caught sight of Olawale picking his way through the acrid smoke and tangled rubble 50 meters away. Samuel's eyes met his father's as Olawale made his way past the white Toyota van that had sat abandoned in the row since early morning.

Samuel muttered a quiet "Thank you Jesus," as he saw his father approaching. It was at that moment that the second, more powerful bomb, which had been hidden inside the van, obliterated life as he knew it.

Having been treated for cuts and lacerations from flying glass and miscellaneous shrapnel, Samuel was released from the chaos of Ola hospital. It was now almost 2 a.m. as he sat alone, numbed and weeping in the darkened front room of the already lonely apartment. He had no idea how he had survived the devastating second blast that had taken his father's life along with friends John, lovely Hannah, and scores of others. The death toll of the two bombings was being officially reported at no fewer than 118 people dead (possibly 200), with countless more injured.[4]

Samuel was overcome by a vast emptiness inside. He had always been a positive person, consistently joyful and optimistic, even in discouraging circumstances but now his heart was consumed by feelings of grief, fear, anger, and worst of all, guilt. He was convinced that his father's death was his fault. If only he had swapped hours with his father, or better yet, offered to work the market for the entire day. He knew that he could no longer stay in Jos, or Nigeria for that matter. Home had become Hell.

Chapter 2

Wrong Number

Abigail Sekibo woke up slightly hung-over and suffering a nasty dry-mouth from last night's clubbing activities. Luanda, the capitol of Angola, offered several attractive clubbing options to choose from. Last night they had selected Palos Disco Club on the *Rue Ferreira* de *Almeida*. It offered a nice change from their usual spot, Lookal Ocean Club, which was more distant, being located at the very tip of Luanda Bay's peninsula. She frequently enjoyed these carefree excursions with her girlfriend and clubbing partner, Yuia. Abigail proceeded to light a Delta mild cigarette just pulled from her clutch purse, then poured herself a small glass of orange juice from the one-room apartment's tiny refrigerator. She quickly snuffed out the just-lit Slovakian made cigarette, deciding that she really didn't want it; it was just an expensive and dirty habit. Abigail had promised herself that she would quit several times before but had not been successful. She would try again soon, she promised.

Abigail had come to realize that, along with her quest to achieve personal independence, she had acquired some unhealthy habits. She was proud though that for the past several years, she had supported herself by taking odd cleaning jobs, selling small trinkets on street corners or doing any manner of work that was offered never once yielding to the temptation of returning home.

For twelve years she had survived on the street, only occasionally being offered temporary sofa space from a kind friend. Today she had her own apartment and depended on no one, especially not a selfish domineering husband. Now, at the age of 30, she had clearly achieved independence but at what cost? She often dreamed of future possibilities, perhaps even marriage. She knew that she would one day want children as well but she was already much older than Angolans considered desirable for producing children. Abigail dated on rare occasion, but preferred to socialize in group settings with friends. She found this less complicated and it helped minimize unwanted advances from sleazy club-scene predators.

Now finished with the application of her makeup, Abigail gazed into the mirror, not displeased with what she saw. She was an attractive woman of thirty. Her bronzed skin, less dark than most and sturdy but curvaceous body, made for a very pleasing package. People often told her that she had pretty features and beautiful smiling eyes. It was obvious though that if she was going to go out with Yuia this weekend, she would need to do something about her hair.

Abigail picked up her purple bejeweled phone and dialed a number she knew by heart. She recognized the accent of the man who picked up.

"This is Abigail," she said, "put Ilene on please."

"No Ilene here. You must have a wrong number," said the voice.

"Stop your fooling with me Omake and put Ilene on. I need to make a hair appointment."

"I'm sorry Miss, there is no Ilene here," replied the man. Abigail knew that it had to be Ilene's husband Omake, because of his distinctive Nigerian accent.

Frustrated with the joking and impatient to reach Ilene, she hung-up and quickly redialed the nine digit number…242-564-3224.

"Hello," said the same Nigerian voice.

"Omake, I'm serious, now give the phone to Ilene," she said impatiently.

"Miss, my name is Samuel Okotie-Eboh and you do have the wrong number."

"Are you sure you are not Omake? You have a Nigerian accent," said Abigail.

"No, I am Angolan" Samuel replied jokingly. "

"No way that you're Angolan. You are for sure from Nigeria."

"Maybe so," he said.

"I'm sorry Samuel. I must have misdialed, good bye then," she said. She sheepishly hung up the phone.

Abigail quickly found her phone book on the bedside table and flipped to Ilene's number. There it was, 242-564-322<u>3</u>; not the 322<u>4</u> she had been so sure of. She carefully dialed the correct number and finally made the appointment.

It was almost a week later when Abigail's phone rang. "This is Samuel, Samuel Okotie-Eboh. We talked briefly when you called my number a few days ago."

"Oh yes, Samuel. Samuel from Nigeria. Sorry again about the wrong number," she said.

"I've been wondering about you ever since you called. "What is your name? You never told me," he asked.

"My name is Abigail Sekibo," she answered.

"Tell me Abigail, how do you speak such good English if you are from Angola," Samuel inquired?

"I have traveled in South Africa many times so my English is pretty good but I am Angolan."

"You sound like a very nice woman," Samuel said shyly, "maybe we can talk again another time. I'd like to get to know you."

"Sure, maybe so", said Abigail as she clicked off the phone. She smiled, finding herself curiously amused by the unexpected phone call. She had met many men in Luanda's coffee shops and bars, but never before through a misdialed phone number.

She stepped out of the shower just in time to hear her phone ring. She quickly wrapped the towel, sarong-like, around her body and grabbed her phone. She knew with certainty who would be calling at this early hour.

"Good morning Samuel." Abigail had begun to look forward to these daily conversations. Somehow they always lifted her spirits.

"Bom dia, (good morning) Abigail," he replied in perfect Portuguese. They commonly switched back and forth from English, the national language of Nigeria, to Portuguese, that of Angola. "We have been speaking now for almost three months and have become good friends."

"I want to meet you. I want to know what you look like."

"No Samuel, you don't want to meet me. I am an old woman and crippled as well," she said jokingly.

"Yes, I want to meet you Abigail even if you are old and crippled," he insisted. "Why don't visit me at my place?"

"No, better if you come to my house. I live in the *Bairro Palanca* area," she said.

"I would never be able to find your house; the streets and houses there all look alike," he replied.

"OK then, we can meet tomorrow in front of *Estadio de Cidadela*. I will be near the entrance facing *Rue da Olivenca* at 3 p.m. I know you can find that!" said Abigail.

Samuel had arranged for a two-hour break from his work today in order to finally meet Abigail. The transmission rebuild could wait a bit for this important occasion. He parked his '03 Nissan XTerra on a side street and walked west toward the stadium entrance. He was understandably excited but more nervous than he had anticipated. He had grown quite fond of the woman ... the voice... on the other end of the phone. What might she think of him, seeing him for the first time? What would she really look like? It now occurred to him that they had not discussed precisely where she would be or what she would be wearing for that matter and the stadium entrance grounds encompassed a huge area.

Samuel approached a nearby bus stop, making his way through the maze of people waiting to board the three o'clock bus. How would he ever pick her out of this crowd? He pulled out his phone to call her. Perhaps he could learn what she was wearing and describe his own attire, bright blue shirt and grey slacks. He dialed the familiar number and placed the phone to his ear, hoping that she would pick up. He heard the familiar ring tone in his ear. It seemed louder than normal. An attractive bronze skinned woman who was standing just in front of him reached to answer her phone.

"Samuel, is that you?" she asked. Samuel, phone still at his ear, gently touched the woman's arm and said,

"Yes, Abigail. It is me!"

"Wow! Abigail, I'm so happy to finally meet you, I mean... *see you*," he said.

"Me too, Samuel," said Abigail, quite pleased to see the fine man that now stood before her.

"Is there a coffee shop or bar near here?" he asked, somewhat shyly.

"Yes," she replied, "it's just a short walk away."

Samuel's two-hour break had passed much too quickly. The newly acquainted pair had been so consumed with their first face-to-face conversation that neither had finished drinking their Fantas. It was already time for Samuel to return to his transmission work and she to her trinket sales. They would plan on meeting again soon.

Abigail was on the bus, returning home from the stadium after meeting with Samuel when her phone rang.

"Hello," she answered, not knowing who might be calling. "Abigail, I love you!"

"What!" she stammered in disbelief.

"I love you. I want to be with you," Samuel professed excitedly.

Stunned at this unexpected declaration, Abigail could only muster. "Thank you Samuel." It had been a long but curiously delightful day.

Chapter 3

A Test of Tolerance

The two had been dating for over two months and were beginning to consider themselves a couple. Abigail had never known or had a relationship with a man like Samuel. He was strong to be sure but also tender and loving. She had never experienced love like that; not from a father, an uncle, or a husband. Samuel treated her with respect — as a partner, but was still very protective of her. Abigail loved that. Through Samuel she was beginning to understand that this *Christian* God, and this *Jesus,* that they followed seemed to have a far different character than the God of *Islam* that she had experienced as a child. This new Christian God was loving, forgiving, protecting much like the attributes that she had come to love in

Samuel. Abigail made the life-changing decision to shed her Muslim heritage and become a Christian. The couple could now begin to envision a future together, but first there were some troublesome issues that must be resolved.

Samuel had been living with his brother since leaving Nigeria following the bombings and the death of their father. Ade, his older brother, had immigrated to Angola one year earlier to escape the increasing violence and political unrest in their homeland. Shortly after joining his brother, Samuel was able to help with expenses, finding work plentiful in the auto packed capitol. The brothers' connection had always been close but recently had deteriorated to the point of becoming unsalvageable.

Ade could not accept this relationship that his younger brother had begun and seemed increasingly determined to make permanent. Even though sweet Abigail had now accepted Christ, she had been raised as a Muslim. Her family was Muslim. Ade's entire family had been driven from their homeland by radical Muslims. They had lost everything, including their father, to the murderous extremists of this evil faith.

Fiercely opposed to this relationship, Ade issued his brother an ultimatum. Samuel was given an impossible choice, either he end this relationship with his formerly Muslim lover or sever his more than 30 year bond with his own brother.

Samuel pulled slowly away from the apartment's parking lot, leaving his familiar assigned space for the last time. The cargo area of the Nissan tightly packed with everything he owned, the front seat piled with shirts still on hangers. His face was still wet from tears as he made the turn onto *Estralla da Catate* heading south to *Bairro Pananca* and Abigail.

Finally, being together with the woman he had come to adore was even better than Samuel could have imagined. He had never known this kind of joy and love, even so, the deep wound from the estrangement with his brother remained painfully raw.

After several months, Samuel had opened a new business, again selling auto parts. The couple depended on each other both financially and emotionally. They both desired children, but so far Abigail had been unsuccessful in becoming pregnant. *In African culture, babies were an expectation of a healthy union. Conversely, it signaled a defective relationship if children were not quickly produced.*

After several trips to the doctor to diagnose the problem, it was discovered that Abigail had only one fallopian tube and that tube had been somehow damaged earlier in life. Pregnancy would likely not be possible for them. The doctors did offer one option, that being a very expensive surgical procedure that *might* provide a slim, perhaps 20% successful, hope of achieving pregnancy.

After learning of this physical inability to conceive, Abigail was becoming increasingly fearful that Samuel might reject her. The medical procedure was extremely costly and it offered too little hope to be seriously considered. She began praying in earnest and desperation to God, this newly discovered Christian God, that he would give them a baby. After all, they had put their faith, their trust in him, not in doctors. Why should these doctors get the glory that only almighty God deserved?

Sensing her fears, Samuel did his best to console her, promising that he would never leave her. They would face this and any future problem together. They would remain united, no matter what.

Perhaps they would adopt a child.

Only six weeks had passed when Abigail was surprised to discover that she was, indeed, now pregnant. God had surely heard her pleas and answered her prayers!

They soon learned that they would be having a boy. Samuel was elated.

Abigail declared, "We will name this baby Saul, which means '*prayed for and given by God.*' Our God deserves all the glory and praise for this miraculous blessing!"

In spite of earlier abuse by her own family and years of alienation, Abigail felt culturally compelled to seek the approval of marriage from the patriarch of the family, Uncle Joao. She arranged for them to meet with the family in order to present the traditional proposal request.

At 7 p.m. on the agreed upon date, they set out on the drive to Abigail's childhood home. Even though it was early evening, the temperature had dropped only a few degrees from the 80⁰ high of the day, with humidity still equaling the temperature, as is typical in May.

"Samuel, please turn on the air conditioner. It is stifling in here." Abigail was thankful for the blessing of cooled air in Samuel's truck. Their home did not have this comfort, nor did most homes in Luanda or most of Africa, for that matter. The route led northeast on the Estrella da *Cacuaco*, and through the city of *Panguila*, and on to *Caxito*, almost one hour's driving time from Luanda. Abigail had not driven this way for almost a dozen years; not since running away to create her own life.

The passing scenery painted the unfortunate picture of life in Luanda. The city had the most expensive cost of living in the world and at the same time was home to a population of greater than 50% unemployed residents. The majority of Angolans subsisted on less than $2 a day.[5]

A short distance out of the city proper, they passed by blocks of unfinished and abandoned residential buildings. Each had been taken over by the poor and now housed multiple families on every floor who had sectioned off their own individual living space.

Abigail was extremely grateful that she and Samuel had been able to live in a modest home and could afford food and transportation. It was not taken for granted that they had been more blessed than many other people in this country.

As they reached *Caxito*, turning left off the main highway and toward her uncle's home, Abigail was becoming more and more anxious.

"Abigail, you seem nervous. Are you OK?" asked Samuel.

"I am much more apprehensive than I expected to be," she answered. "I thought that I could block out all the memories and just focus on getting through it. It's not working," The wounds and fears, which she had tried for years to bury, were returning in a flood. She could only imagine what kind of reception they might receive.

Approaching the entry, Abigail abruptly let go of Samuels's hand, thinking that such ordinary display of affection might not find favor in this house.

Tradition demanded that all family members be present for the *alambamento or bride price (*the asking for the hand in marriage). This rite was often considered more important than the civil ceremony itself. Samuel would be required to pay the family a sum of money, typically $300 to $500, as compensation for the valuable asset, the amount to be determined by the uncle, as well as to purchase a list of additional items of the uncle's choosing. Such a list might include a new suit for the uncle or other specifically requested gifts for other family members.

In his case, Samuel expected the bride payment to be inflated, as he had "jumped through the window," a term used in this culture to describe a prospective groom who had made the bride-to-be pregnant before the wedding.[6]

The couple was greeted at the door and ushered into the large central room by a young man, probably a nephew. Abigail did not recognize him after so many years, but nothing had changed inside the home; same dusty pictures on the wall, a gold filigree covered Quran displayed on its pedestal and open to the same page that she remembered from thirty years before, same curtains, now more faded, covering the room's small windows. Even the lingering odor from the cooking of tonight's *galinha de cabidela* (chicken and garlic rice) dinner seemed familiar. Abigail remembered that she, along with all the females of the house, had always been required to eat in the kitchen, separated from her uncle and other male family members who ate in the dining room.

Her aunt, rising from the chair where she had been seated, approached to meet them, giving Abigail a formal but cold kiss on her cheek. Her uncle remained stoically seated in the large formal chair that she remembered all too well. It had seemed like "the throne of a tyrant" when she was a girl. All the other family members, now staring back with older versions of once familiar faces, were seated around the room's perimeter.

Samuel, who was unsuccessful in concealing his discomfort, had just begun to present his letter of request when Uncle Joao abruptly leapt from his chair. Now face to face with Samuel, he shouted, "There will be no marriage to this woman! You are Christian and we will not accept you into this family."

He was now angrily gesturing toward Abigail. "She is still the wife of another husband and is now pregnant with a bastard child! She has defiled herself, brought disgrace on her family, and is not worthy and now she has become a Christian. I am sure that you do not know of her many sins." Her uncle then proceeded to pour out, to a stunned Samuel, a full accounting of Abigail's unsavory history and ugly details of her young life and failed marriages.

Again, Abigail was feeling terrified that Samuel would reject her, certainly now knowing of her earlier marriages and troubled history.

The couple began the long drive home in silence, neither knowing what to say, or for Samuel, even what he was feeling. Abigail, quietly sobbing, began to speak.

"Samuel, I am so very sorry that I never told you the truth about my past. I was afraid that you would no longer want to be with me if you knew. My uncle did not tell you the full truth. Please let me explain." With that, Abigail began to tell Samuel her story.

There had always seemed a dark shadow over her life. Her early years had been a nightmare best forgotten, none the less, she would often revisit those horrible times in order to revive the strength and resolve needed to overcome more current challenges.

The worst had begun when she was just seven years old. Her father had given her away to her uncle, following the unexpected death of her mother to be raised along with her uncle's children.

Her family was strict Muslim, the minority, in overwhelmingly Christian Angola.

In her uncle's home, she was treated like a slave, abused and relegated to endless cleaning, cooking, and the most unpleasant jobs, while the naturally born daughters did little. The others attended a private school, while Abigail, alone, was placed in an inferior government school.

She was only eleven when the mutilation was performed. Abigail's grandmother (uncle's mother), had taken her to a rear bedroom where she was forced to strip naked and then bound with legs spread open. Using a special knife and a razor blade, the grandmother began to slice away her clitoris and tissue of the labia minora, this all without the use of an anesthetic. This barbaric practice (female *circumcision),* common in many Islamic Northern African and Arabic countries, is frequently associated with Islam but is not officially endorsed by either Muslim or Christian religion. In Abigail's community it was expected as a prerequisite to marriage. The reality was that it resulted from a long history of gender inequality. The purpose was to control a woman's sexuality (the procedure often rendered the girl unable to experience pleasure) while supposedly enhancing the pleasure of the husband.[7]

The event had left Abigail severely scared, both physically and emotionally. Long after she had healed and was again able to walk without bleeding or discomfort, she still burned with resentment. She understood that she had become nothing more than a family commodity to be bartered for and sold against her will.

Abigail continued. She was fourteen when her uncle, exerting his *Wali mujbir* authority *(guardian who is permitted to force marriage)*, announced that she would soon be forced to marry a man she had never met.[8] She had no choice in the matter. For this arranged contract, her uncle had received a very handsome sum from the groom, even though the payment of *mehr* (dowry) was intended by Islamic law, to become the property of the bride.[9] The husband to be, much older than her own father, already had three existing wives and numerous children. Abigail's desperate pleadings of opposition to her uncle did nothing to prevent the polygamous union from taking place.

Over the following two years, she endured daily abuse from both the husband and the more senior wives. Living in slave-like conditions, her life seemed dark and without hope.

Abigail finally made the decision to run away from this toxic existence, returning to Joao's home where he reluctantly allowed her to stay.

Once again, at age eighteen, she was forced into marriage with a friend of her uncle. Here she suffered even more abuse, this time more physical than before. She had become pregnant, finally fulfilling the primary expectation of their African culture. After a particularly brutal beating, Abigail lost the baby.

She had run away again, for good this time, to the streets of Luanda. Could it be any worse than life had been under the iron hand and unloving authority of her uncle's family or her husbands?

They had nearly reached home by the time Abigail had finished telling her story. Samuel had said nothing over the entire drive, listening, but giving no indication of his reaction to the tearful narrative. Abigail was fearing the worst. Samuel parked the Nissan in its usual space, let himself out and walked around the front to open Abigail's door, helping her out as he always had done. As she stood, Samuel grasped her face in his hands and he wept. "Abigail, I am so very sorry! I did not know of your suffering and heartache. I love you. I love you Abigail Sekibo … and you *will* become my wife!"

Two months before the birth of their son Saul, Abigail and Samuel were finally married in a simple civil ceremony. They had learned that contrary to what

Abigail's guardians had insisted, the holy book of Islam, the Quran, although it **did** permit the taking of multiple wives, it did **not** allow for marriage to be forced upon either partner. "**O ye who believe!** *Ye are forbidden to inherit women against their will.* Nor should ye treat them with harshness that ye may take away part of the dower [money given by the husband to the wife for the marriage contract] ye have given them, except where they have been guilty of open lewdness; on the contrary live with them on a footing of kindness and equity. If ye take a dislike to them it may be that ye dislike a thing, and God brings about through it a great deal of good." (The Noble Quran, 4:19) [10]

Abigail's *forced* marriages could therefore be considered invalid! The civilized world would have likely labeled these events crimes of torture or even rape.

Abigail and Samuel were grateful for their next two years together, happily watching their beautiful little boy grow and thankful to be united in a loving, healthy marriage; however, with each successive news report they became more fearful of continuing to live their lives in Angola. A future here that included safety and security for their family was appearing increasingly hopeless.

Nearly three previous decades of civil war had ended in 2002, leaving almost one million people dead and another four million displaced. Many of those had been forcibly resettled without land, basic resources, or even identification documents. The resettlement process was slowed by the presence of an estimated 500,000 land mines which left large tracts of the country inaccessible to humanitarian aid. The twenty-seven-year conflict had forced more than another half-million to flee to neighboring countries.[11]

Petty bribery was widespread with city officials, including the police, requiring the payment of "*gasosas*, the local term for bribes," in order to move any simple civil action along or to be released from fabricated crimes. The long-time president (thirty-five years) of Angola, José Eduardo dos Santos, had been accused of corruption for decades. Somehow under his leadership more than 25% of Angola's oil revenues had gone missing. Curiously, his oldest daughter Isabel had suddenly become Africa's richest woman, mysteriously banking more than three billion dollars.[12]

Even now, eight years later, fundamental rights such as freedom of expression and information had become curtailed, despite strong guarantees in the new constitution. In the first half of the year, an estimated 25,000 residents were forcibly evicted from their homes in Huila, without compensation or prior notice and resettled in peripheral areas without any infrastructure, driving many into extreme poverty. Just last month, the government had ordered the destruction of at least 3,000 residences in Lubango to clear land for railway lines, and in just the past three months, demolished at least another

1,500 houses to make way, supposedly, for an urban beautification project.[13]

Throughout the long civil war, rebel groups had been largely funded by the sales of Blood (or conflict) Diamonds. Even though the fields were now under government control, horrific abuses were continuing.

It had been reported that during the last year, government soldiers massacred over 200 people in their effort to control the diamond fields in the east of the country. They raped local women and, using the threat of violence, forced peasants into mining work.[14]

It was not war that seemed to be spreading across Africa like a pandemic, but it was an unstoppable wave of heavily armed banditry fueled by evil. Africa had not experienced this level of violence since the years of the 80's when war lords like Joseph Kony of the LRA committed their atrocities in Uganda. Now with Boko Haram committing undiscriminating murder of thousands in central Africa, the political upheaval of military coups in Guinea and Madagascar, and the increasing gang violence in the oil-polluted Niger Delta, it seemed there would be no end to the brutality. Additionally, the Eastern Congo was experiencing an epidemic of rape with armed groups of men sexually and sadistically assaulting thousands of women.

In the couple's home country of Angola, 150,000 children each year were starving. At the same time,

Luanda's corrupt elite lived in $10,000 a month apartments flowing with champagne and wearing diamonds mined in bloody fields.[15]

Baby Saul, now a little over two years old, was such a beautiful little child. He lay there sleeping peacefully in his tiny bed, wearing his favorite red and black batman pajamas, and oblivious to the life altering discussion that had just concluded in his parents' bedroom. Luanda, Angola and all of Africa itself, had become far too corrupt, too dangerous, too hopeless, for this baby, this precious family, to remain. There would be no future here.

In the Bible's book of Psalms, David wrote of *"The valley of the shadow of death"* — that *"shadow of death"* had now overtaken Angola, Nigeria, Somalia, and much of Africa.

Samuel and Abigail made the heart-wrenching decision. They would leave everything and everyone that they had known and leave Africa forever.

Chapter 4

Flight from Fear

The total combined flying time from Luanda's *Quatro de Fevereiro Airport* to their destination of Sao Paulo, Brazil, would be almost twenty hours, with one plane change in Casablanca, Morocco. A non-stop flight direct from Luanda would have been only eight and one-half hours, but would have been impossibly expensive for the young family. As it was, Samuel and Abigail had put away every last kwanza for the past six months, sold Samuel's Nissan, and liquidated all the assets of the auto parts business in order to buy the tickets for the three of them. They were taking with them only what they could stuff into their two large roller bags plus a large duffle for

Saul. Even the majority of Saul's treasured toys had been left behind.

In considering a new country that could offer a young family both safety and opportunity, Brazil would not have been their first choice. They had much preferred seeking citizenship in the U.S. or Canada, but visa applications for those options had been rejected. In Brazil, at least their skin color and language (Portuguese) would be the norm.

With their bags stuffed beneath them, the trip to the airport was hectic and sweaty, but typical for a fully loaded microbus taxi ride. Abigail and Samuel were perspiring profusely by the time they reached the airport, and they were grateful to get themselves and their baby into the cooler air inside the terminal.

Their departing flight, AT290, was with Morocco's *Royal Air Maroc* airline, not the best or quickest, but certainly the least expensive option. They would fly in the economy section for the long trip. The first leg to Morocco, flying completely the opposite direction from their final destination in Brazil, would take six hours and forty minutes with a layover of one and a half hours before continuing on flight AT213, the nearly twelve additional hours to Sao Paulo.

After checking their bags, other than the small carry-on filled with essentials needed for Saul, the family patiently shuffled through the agonizingly slow moving security line. Patience was a quality that was necessary in order to preserve one's emotional health in this country.

Having now passed successfully through security, the couple could now feel a bit less anxious. It was not uncommon for travelers to be harassed over their documents and made to pay a *fee* (gasosa) to be permitted entry.

"Another blessing from you today God!" Samuel thought to himself.

After settling into three adjacent seats in the waiting area of gate 14B, Abigail turned her attention to Saul. The two-year-old toddler had been amazingly good so far but he was now becoming visibly tired and hungry. Abigail removed two plastic bags from the plump blue carry-on, one filled with sliced mango, Saul's favorite snack, and the other with a dozen or so *Nuttikrust* (toffee flavored) biscuits. This would satisfy the boy's hunger for now but she could only hope that he would sleep for much of the exhausting trip ahead.

With the baby momentarily content and currently occupied with an admiring woman in the seat next to him, Samuel and Abigail could finally take a breath. Samuel leaned over to Abigail and softly kissing her cheek whispered, "I love you Abi. We will be alright."

Samuel, though wanting to comfort his wife, was himself apprehensive. He had never flown before as Abigail had — a couple of short flights within South Africa — but now he needed to show confidence, he needed to protect, to lead. He must be strong.

"Flight AT290 to Casablanca will be boarding shortly," said a pleasant voice over the loudspeaker.

"We will be taking passengers that require assistance and families with small children first."

Gently taking her little boy's arm, Abigail said, "It's time to go for our ride on the big airplane, baby."

As they waited near the gate's window to board, they entertained Saul, pointing out the plane's colorful markings, tasteful green and red strips below the windows extending the full length of its bright white body, and a large green star logo with a red elliptical swoosh emblazoned on the huge tail.

Within a few short minutes, the family had boarded the huge Boeing 767-300ER airliner, found their way to row 21 immediately behind the more expensive economy plus section and set about buckling a wide-eyed Saul into his seat between them. Seats C, E, and H had no window views, but the larger center aisle did allow them to be seated together.

Samuel removed his phone from his front pocket and dialed a number that had not been dialed in almost three years. The number rang twice and immediately switched to voice mail.

Samuel, after taking a long deep breath, spoke, "Ade, this is your brother, Samuel. We are on an airplane headed to Brazil. We are leaving Angola for good — I — you — are my brother Ade — I love you. Goodbye Ade."

Samuel sat with eyes closed as remaining passengers filed by, making their way to their economy seats further rear. Feeling a gentle touch on his forearm, he accepted the tissue that Abigail offered and wiped the tears from his eyes.

With its twin turbofan engines roaring at full power, the 767 wide-body lifted off the hot Angolan tarmac and began a steep climb west, then at 20,000 feet altitude and still climbing, began a turn northwest over the South Atlantic Ocean. Samuel's right hand was still firmly gripping his armrest while the left gently stroked his son's thigh. Silently, he mouthed the words of his favorite Bible verse, Jeremiah 29:11.

"For I know the plans I have for you," declares the LORD *"plans to prosper you and not to harm you, plans to give you hope and a future."*

Samuel could only pray that God would be faithful in this promise. The young family's trust had now been placed fully in his hands.

The plane touched down at Casablanca's Mohammed V International Airport 10 minutes early thanks to favorable winds. It was night time, 9 p.m. now with the time zone difference, as flight AT290 rolled up to terminal two's gate 232. The weary couple, with their very sleepy toddler held securely in Samuel's arms made their way into the seemingly endless and brightly illuminated expanse of arrival corridor "E".

At this hour, the busiest airport hub in North Africa was uncrowded and quiet. Abigail, having previous flying experience, scanned the departure display board to determine the gate number for their plane change. Samuel, feeling unusually anxious and disoriented, was more than happy to let her lead. Of course the departure gate for AT213 to Sao Paulo would be the furthest option away, being located at the far end of corridor "D". Samuel was now grateful for every minute of the 90-minute layover time.

It was 7:25 a.m. when the family arrived at Sao Paulo International. The 7540 km distance had taken a very long twelve hours. The morning skies over the Guarulhos area were partly cloudy and the taxiways were still wet from a recent shower. The couple was relieved and excited to finally reach, what would hopefully become, their new home — but they were also filled with great apprehension. Once outside this aircraft, they would be entering a new world, a new life, an environment of complete unknowns, and they must still pass through the uncertainty of Brazil's immigration checkpoint.

Saul was fully awake and was suffering a serious case of "cabin fever" as they deplaned. Abigail struggled to contain him as they walked through the arrival area and followed the somewhat intimidating signage, which directed all *non-citizens* to passport control. Each of the half-dozen or so document stations was manned by a uniformed immigration officer, all displaying equally serious and impersonal facial expressions.

The family did carry current passports and visas as required, but they had applied for travel visas which authorized only a *brief* stay in the country. Fearful of rejection, they had not truthfully indicated their long-term intensions. Samuel was keenly aware that the officers might show suspicion since a great many Africans before them had illegally entered the country with just such limited visas, only to quickly disappear into the staggering population of Sao Paulo's twenty million residents.

Attempting to appear calm, the couple handed their papers to the officer at their station. The officer studied the documents while he typed entries into his computer. Seeming suddenly concerned, he compared the papers again with the information on his display screen. He studied Abigail and Samuel intently and then turned his attention to Saul. "Is the boy actually your son? Where was he born?"

"Yes, of course he is our son. He is two years old and was born October 4th, 2013, at Americo Boavida Hospital in Luanda," Abigail stated emphatically.

"Why would you choose to bring a small boy on such a visit?" asked the skeptical officer.

"We had no family in Luanda who could care for him, so we had no choice," Abigail replied.

Samuel, heart now racing with fear, was beginning to perspire. Excruciating seconds ticked by. Nodding, to alert the next traveler in line, the officer abruptly stamped the three sets of documents and impatiently waved the grateful family through. They secured their papers and their little boy as they moved hurriedly down the hallway toward baggage claim. As they approached the baggage conveyors, Samuel heard a voice call out behind him. "You there. Stop!" shouted the voice.

Samuel's heart pounded in his chest. He turned to look back, hoping the order was not intended for them. He stiffened as he saw the uniformed man running directly toward them.

Offering the small stuffed bunny to Saul, the skycap, still breathing heavily, said, "Your son dropped this at the immigration counter."

"Oh, thank you so much!" Abigail replied, sounding genuinely relieved, "that was so very kind of you," she continued, as the man had already turned back and disappeared into the crowd.

An hour later, the family had secured their bags and had found the least costly transportation that could take them to their destination near the *Centro* district of Sao Paulo. For the fare of 5.60 BRL (Brazilian Real or $1.50 US dollars), the city's subway system, commonly called the Metro, offered service departing every half hour for the 40 minute trip to the *Tatuape* (bus/subway station) which was 25 km (16 miles) away. Abigail's Angolan friend, Ama

Mgbeoji, their one and only contact on the continent, had found them a temporary place to stay near the old center of the city.

Neither Abigail nor Samuel had ever ridden on a subway, or traveled underground at all, so this trip on Metro 299 would be just one more stressful experience. Saul, on the other hand, was glued to the window, seemingly mesmerized by the streaming view of strobe-like flashes of light alternating with dark and undiscernible features as the train sped through the tunnel.

Abigail was grateful for Ana, whom had befriended her many years earlier, soon after she ran away to the streets of Luanda. Ana had found refuge in Brazil two years earlier and she was now settled in central Sao Paulo. She was able to reserve a small apartment in advance for the family near her own by agreeing to act as their *fiador* (rental guarantor).

Arriving at Tatuape's busy terminal, the family exited the Metro below ground and proceeded to climb the stairway up one level to the bus station, not an easy task while carrying a small boy, two very heavy suitcases, and Saul's bag. Samuel soon identified a local bus that would take them the remaining distance, about 8 km southeast, to Sapopemba, one of the least expensive neighborhoods of Sao Paulo. Sapopemba was considered a *cortico* (slum tenement) neighborhood, but offered far better living conditions than the even poorer *favelas* (shantytowns), which housed over 20% of the city's population. The family was preparing to begin their new life in extremely humbling conditions.[16]

Chapter 5

A New Beginning

Abigail's reunion with Ama was both tearful and joyful. She was there to greet the family upon arrival and help with their orientation to the new surroundings. The apartment she had located for the family consisted of a single, large, furnished room. Within its green painted walls were one double bed, a small table with two wooden chairs, a floor lamp without a shade, and a tiny two burner gas stove. Bathroom facilities would be shared with the five other building tenants. This particular *cortico* apartment had been created from the partitioning of a large, older two-story home unlike the majority in Sapopemba, which were created from subdivisions of abandoned factory, industrial or hotel interiors. The apartment even had a small window — a rare amenity in this type of residence. Ama had done well!

The couple's housing quality in Luanda had certainly been superior, but they had anticipated that starting over in a new country would require sacrifice. They were highly motivated and industrious. Brazil would offer such people new opportunities to improve their lives and thrive.

Their remaining savings, nearly $1,000, would have to last until they could find work. First thing tomorrow, Abigail would pursue a promising lead that Ama had suggested, while Samuel cared for Saul.

By 7 a.m. Abigail had joined the ethnic stew of *Paulistanos*, as residents of Sao Paulo are called, on a dark green and white transit bus bound for the old *Centro* district, a fairly short, 8 km away. This was Abigail's first real view of the city. Sao Paulo, the largest city in the Southern hemisphere, was packed with more than twelve million people, an estimated four million automobiles, and block after block of decaying but fully occupied buildings, colorful small shops, and corner food markets. Almost every wall and vertical surface was covered with the Brazilian graffiti known as *pichacao*, a cryptic style resembling the ancient runic writing of Scandinavia.

It was difficult to imagine that more than 70% of Sao Paulo's 20 million residents lived in just such substandard housing, while the rich elite lived in high rise mansions and traversed the city, hopping rooftop to rooftop, by personal helicopter. Sao Paulo's 240 helipads easily outnumbered New York's meager 10.

Abigail stepped off the bus at the intersection of *R. Vitoria* and *Av. São João*. Ama had provided perfect directions. Many of the building walls were covered with posters advertising evangelical Christian events, which seemed in contrast to the dozens of drug-addicted locals who appeared to be living on the street. She continued one block east and made a left turn onto *Alameda Barão de Limeira*. Just 20 meters down the street on the left, she spotted a window with large bold red letters reading, "Biyou'Z, specializing in African cuisine". This was the place.

Even before she had stepped through the door, the atmosphere felt familiar. The conversations tinged with accents of Lingal, Mozambican, Angolan, Swahili, and English, and the familiar smells of African cooking were unmistakable. The owners, Macaia Victor a local, and Melanito Biyouha, originally from Cameroon, had opened the restaurant six years earlier hoping to find an audience with Sao Paulo's huge and growing African population. It had since achieved that goal, and more, becoming a central fixture in what had become known as the city's *African Corner*. Since that time, two more Nigerian restaurants had opened just down the street.[17]

Abigail entered the dining room and seated herself at one of the many yellow-and-white checkered cloth covered tables. The room was alive with animated conversations and patrons who sat drinking freshly brewed coffee and scanning today's *Folha de São Paulo* news. The interior decor was simple. Its bright salmon-pink walls, decorated with traditional African wooden masks, created a warm and welcoming atmosphere. The wall opposite the tiny kitchen was adorned with a huge map of Africa, which had begun to yellow with age, and was covered with the signatures of hundreds of visiting immigrants who had proudly autographed their former homelands.

An attractive woman, perhaps in her early 40's and wearing a beautiful beige head wrap, patterned with black and terra cotta markings, popped out of the kitchen carrying a steaming platter of *akara* (delicious deep fried bean cakes) and a side of fresh baked *agege* bread. The woman carried herself like "the woman in charge," so Abigail was certain that this must be the owner, Melinito. She delivered the food to grateful customers, then turned to greet Abigail, who she had quickly spotted.

"*Bom Dia Senhorita* (good morning Miss), what would you like this morning?" Melinito inquired in Cameroonian accented Portuguese.

"Coffee please, with cream," answered Abigail. "And I hope to speak with you when you have a moment."

"Of course sweetie," she said with a big smile, disappearing back into the kitchen.

Melinito returned in a flash with two mugs of coffee, a small pitcher of cream, two slices of hot *agege* bread, and sat down across from Abigail.

"The bread is on the house," she said. "I haven't eaten anything this morning, so please join me."

"Thank you Melinito, I recognized you at once from my friend Ama's description, my name is Abigail Sekibo."

"Oh yes, of course! Ama has spoken so highly of you and had told me that you might be coming by."

The two women chatted for nearly an hour, in spite of the frequent interruptions for the store owner to attend to her customers. The conversation went surprisingly well, and Melinito quickly understood why Abigail had been so highly recommended.

"Abigail, several people before you have applied for this server position, but I *really* like you. Could you begin work on Monday?"

Of course, Abigail would be overjoyed to accept and to begin work on Monday!

Until Samuel could also find work, and hopefully very soon, he would need to assume the role of Mr. Mom, with fulltime duties of cooking, cleaning, and care of their son. Samuel had always been such a wonderful father and husband. Abigail had no doubt that he would be up to the task.

The couple was just beginning to understand the complex culture and history that had resulted in Brazil's current environment. It had been 500 years since Portuguese traders had first introduced African slaves into Brazil. Afro-Brazilians, most knowing very little of African culture or history, now made up 53% of the population, the largest black population outside of Africa. Like Samuel and Abigail, the recent flood of African immigrants, along with others from Europe, Asia, and

Central America came seeking work in the expanding economy and refuge from violence and war. Many came without visas, some seeking asylum, but all were subject to prejudices of race, color, and the false but common assumption that most of them were uneducated.

Brazil's color or racial distinctions fell into four main ethnic groups: Indian, White, Black (*Preta*), and Yellow (Mongoloid Asian). Those who were of mixed race were considered *Pardo*, which itself was broken into five more designations depending on racial mix. Even though slavery had been abolished in 1888, black and darker skinned individuals, *Pretas*, were still much more often victims of poverty and underrepresentation in higher levels of government, military service and business, while the population's whiter, or light skinned people, seemed to enjoy unrestricted opportunity.[18]

"Yes," Abigail thought, "there are many difficulties here, but there is no war — no Boko Haram — no shadow. We can have a life in this country."

It was a Thursday in early February, 52 days before Easter, and the atmosphere in the Centro district was energized with anticipation of *Carnival*. Tomorrow afternoon would mark the beginning of the nearly week long celebration.

Sao Paulo's Carnival was not quite as huge as that of Rio de Janeiro, but it was still the most famous holiday and biggest happening of the year. Thousands of people, including foreigners, had flooded into the city and were gearing up to party during the non-stop day and night festivities.

Thanks to the hordes of hungry revelers, this week would be *Biyou' Z's* most profitable week of the year. The restaurant was already packed with customers who were enjoying plates of Melinito's famous *fumbua* (fried chicken in roasted peanut sauce, palm oil, crushed dried shrimp and manioc) or the other big favorite, *ndolé*, (Cameroon's national dish, a spicy stew of bitter greens, meat, and peanuts, served with fried plantains).

Abigail had never seen anything like it but one thing was certain— business at Biyou' Z was "off the charts," her tips were amazing and she and Samuel had been given a generous gift from Melinito and Macaia!

Tomorrow they would be joining countless thousands of spectators at Sao Paulo's famous *Anhembi Sambadrome* to watch the event's first of five days of samba competition. The grandstand tickets costing 122 BR ($34) were the least expensive available, with premier tickets topping out at 5,858 BRL ($1,625) each. None the less, Abigail and Samuel were extremely grateful for the unexpected gift.

The couple had left home at 6 p.m. in order to catch the crowded Metro which would take them to Tiete station, a short walk away from the huge Sambadrome. Saul had been left with their friend Ama's 16-year-old son,

Guelo, who had become his frequent sitter. Saul had come to regard him like a big brother. Guelo was such a fine young man and was so gentle and protective with their boy that Abigail and Samuel always felt comfortable leaving Saul in his care.

The walk from the station to *Anhembi* was only a few blocks away, and Samuel was grateful to be walking within a crowd of people who shared the same destination. The city was plagued by dangerous gangs of gun toting young men who frequently preyed on victims of opportunity, committing robbery and beatings, when not engaged in their primary money making activity, the selling of drugs and weapons. These gangs had members as young as 10 or 12 years old, who were often surprisingly violent, and could be especially nervous and unpredictable.

The couple found their section, number 2, located at the very start of the 500-meter-long, grandstand lined, parade route. The stands, which also serve as start-finish for the Brazilian Grand Prix Formula 1 race, held in November, accommodates up to 26,000 spectators and was already approaching capacity 30 minutes before start time.

At precisely 20:00 hours, with driving beats of tribal-like rhythms filling the air, the first of 13 competing samba schools, Águia de Ouro, exploded into movement.[19] Both the music and the dancer's outrageous costumes owed their heritage to the influence of former African slaves that were traded into Brazil from 1600 to

1888. Abigail found it ironic that this huge spectacle, now being celebrated as a *Brazilian* cultural celebration, had actually been imported, along with slaves from her own country of Angola, in the 1800's.

The scantily-clad samba dancers, all beautiful, shapely, young women, were costumed in nothing more than strategically placed strands of beads, sequins, and feathers. The dancers were costumed in their particular school's colors, with Águia de Ouro's dancers costumed in their colors of blue, gold, and white. Their bejeweled headdresses sprouted fans of immense feather plumes which vibrated wildly to every pulsing move. With the abundance of exposed flesh and provocative dancing, it was curious that this festival would have had its roots in Christianity.

According to some, the carnival was originally a Greek spring festival in honor of the god of wine, Dionysus. The Romans adopted the same tradition with a feast in honor of Bacchus, the Roman god of wine, and Saturnalia. On this day master and slaves exchanged clothes amidst a day full of drunken revelry. The Roman Catholic Church later modified the feast of Saturnalia into a festival preceding the beginning of Lent. The festival, however, evolved into a mass celebration of indulgences in music, dance, food, and drink, something which the Church did not have in mind.[20] Aside from fasting from eating meat, there appeared to be no clear connection.

The next several hours became a sensory blur of non-stop dancing, music, color, and elaborately decorated floats, followed by even more impressive performances from the other samba teams. The stands shook with every drum beat, as spectators danced and celebrated along with the nearly-nude parade dancers.

Abigail and Samuel were enjoying this new cultural experience, especially the music, the dance, and color, but they couldn't help but be shocked by the public celebration of sexuality and exposed flesh. Though neither of them considered themselves to be prudes, they found the raucous atmosphere challenging to their conservative African sensibilities.

Chapter 6

A Rough Start

Thanks to a great recommendation from Melinito, Samuel had found work as a server at Centro's *Nigeriano* restaurant, conveniently located only one-half block from *Biyou'Z* on *Rua Vitória*. It was no accident that the chosen location was so close to Melinito's establishment, as there were now three Nigerian restaurants located strategically close to the well-established anchor business, Biyou'Z.

Samuel had hoped to launch another business doing automotive repair and parts sales as he had done before in Nigeria and Angola; however, circumstances in Sapopemba, combined with the lack of a car, made that impossible at this time. His income from the serving job was less than he would be making in the auto business, but it did allow him to alternate his schedule with Abigail's in order to provide continual care for Saul.

It was nearly 1 a.m. by the time that Samuel stepped off the bus after returning home from his work shift at the restaurant.

Nigeriano had hosted dinner for a special private party, requiring Samuel to work long beyond normal closing time, and he was anxious to get home for the night.

He walked the two long blocks along *Rue Tecala*, and then turned right, beginning the climb up the steep hill that led to the family's apartment.

The black Lexus sedan was totally out of place on this street. Cars of this quality were not uncommon in Sao Paulo's business district but were rarely seen in an area like *Sapobemba* — especially near the *favela*. The car set parked, hood open, in the dirt just off the crumbling asphalt. The exquisitely dressed owner stood next to the driver-side door loudly cursing into his cell phone at some unfortunate individual on the receiving end of the call.

It was obvious that the $80,000+ GS-F luxury car, had experienced some problem, and the driver was left stranded.

Although it was dark and the area had no street lights, there was sufficient light coming from a neighborhood bar nearby to illuminate the scene.

Samuel was exhausted, and was tempted to walk on by, but he was too kind and mechanically gifted to pass by without offering his assistance.

"Looks like your car has a problem. Can I give you any help?" Samuel inquired.

"The expensive piece of s--- just stopped on me," the irritated man replied. "I called for someone to pick me up, but it will take them at least a half-hour to get here."

"Probably nothing I can do, but I can take a look at it if you like. I know a little bit about cars," Samuel said. "And besides, Lexus is really an expensive Toyota. I have worked on hundreds of Toyotas."

"Sure *meu amigo* — be my guest! I have a flashlight in my glovebox that you can use."

Samuel took the flashlight and inspected the engine compartment for any obvious clues to the problem. The Lexus was brand new and the engine was covered by the typical plastic shroud that *aesthetically* concealed most mechanical components on these late model cars.

As Samuel swept the light over the battery box, he spotted a suspicious looking battery terminal connection. He twisted the connector and found it to be loose, as he suspected.

"*Senhor*, I think I have found your problem—a loose battery connector. These roads are too rough and the vibration often causes such connectors to loosen. It's an easy fix, but I will need to walk to my home to get a wrench."

"I will be happy to pay you handsomely if you can do that!" the driver exclaimed.

"No worries, I would be happy to help!" Samuel replied. "I will return in about 15 minutes; my house is only a short distance up the hill."

Just as he promised, Samuel returned with the crescent wrench *(his professional tools had been sold before leaving Angola)* and quickly had the connector tightened on the battery post.

The car's anxious owner switched on the ignition and successfully started the car.

"Please, let me pay you for your help *amigo*," the grateful man offered, pulling a large roll of bills from his pocket.

"No, no, I cannot accept payment for this small service," Samuel declared, "I'm sure that you will do the same for someone else when you have the opportunity."

"You are a very good man, my friend! If you will not accept my money let me give you something of perhaps more value. I am a person of significant influence in this city. Most of this influence is unknown to others, but believe me, I have great influence with the police, with judicial officials, everyone." With that, the man offered Samuel some very useful and privileged information.

Today Samuel was home with Saul, and they were walking the 2 km to the large market on *R. Barão de Ladário*. Saul was now 2 years old and with the family not owning a car, he had become accustomed to walking substantial distances with his mother and father. The walk to the market was almost a daily necessity since their small apartment had only a very small refrigerator, but Samuel looked forward to the time outdoors with his boy and saw it as an opportunity for them both to get some exercise.

The massive *Mercado Municipal* was easily the most imposing structure on the busy one-way street. Its unusual brown-colored masonry and cathedral-like architecture, complete with ornate patina-copper roof dome, easily set it apart from the surrounding businesses. Contributing to the building's cathedral-like appearance were rows of intricately designed stained glass windows that were built into the building's high walls. The interior's peaked ceiling reached nearly 20 meters in height and was supported by two dozen ornately-decorated stone colonnades. Although the structure had ample artificial illumination, the majority of light came from beautiful lattice paneled skylights in the cavernous ceiling.

Samuel typically used the shopping errand as an opportunity to entertain Saul. Today, after purchasing the chicken, plantains, and milk that had been on their list, they strolled between rows of vendor stalls which were overflowing with colorful displays of fruit and fresh produce. Samuel let Saul select a small watermelon, which pleased the boy greatly, then stopped at a rolling cart to get an ice cream—vanilla for himself and chocolate for Saul, before setting out on the walk home.

Weather permitting, Samuel liked to walk a few blocks out of the way so that Saul could enjoy some playtime at a small community park near the *Brás* Metro Station. Green spaces like this were very rare in the crowded city, so Samuel loved these opportunities for his boy to experience an environment other than asphalt and concrete. It was early evening and with plenty of light remaining, the two made the detour towards the park.

The daily homebound rush of Metro commuters had already passed so the park nearby was virtually empty. Samuel and Saul would have some rare time to enjoy the park by themselves. Samuel sat down on one of the park's wooden benches, placed his grocery bag on the ground next to him, and sat contentedly watching Saul, who was focused on climbing onto the back of a huge concrete turtle in a sandbox nearby.

The little boy was a happy child but often seemed lonely. Saul very much wanted a baby brother or sister and he made that known constantly. Both Abigail and Samuel wanted another child, but it seemed that the problems with Abigail's reproductive system would not allow a second pregnancy. They hadn't given up hope and continued to pray that God would grant them a second child, just as he had granted them the miracle two years earlier with baby Saul. Perhaps he would answer their prayers once again.

As soon as he spotted the group of young men emerge from behind a wall at the edge of the park, Samuel knew that they could be trouble. The oldest of the boys appeared to be around 18, with several perhaps as young as 11-12 years old. They carried themselves with the unmistakable swagger of favela "hustlers," or gang members. These juvenile gangs were active in virtually all of Sao Paulo's favelas and were extremely territorial. The sales of drugs and guns made them rich, powerful, and dangerous. Most favela gangs had a military-like command structure, with one *dono* in charge of the managers and soldiers *(soldados)* within their territory. Both the civil police and military police routinely accepted bribes to allow gang activities to go unnoticed so most gangs operated with impunity.[21]

Anticipating the threat, Samuel jumped to his feet and started toward Saul, who was still playing about 30 meters away.

"Ei, cara" (Hey dude), shouted one of the older boys. Samuel, ignoring the boy, continued toward his son.

"Você, filho de puta!" (You, son of a bitch!).

This time, Samuel stopped and turned to face the pack of boys. He knew that they carried guns and were often quick to use them.

"O que você quer?" (What do you want?), Samuel replied in an attempt to act unconcerned. "All we have is a few groceries."

One of the smaller boys had grabbed the bag from near the bench and was already dumping its contents out on the ground. The milk was still cold, so several of the boys took a few gulps, passing the carton among themselves, while they finished off the plantains.

Saul did not understand what was happening, but sensed something wrong. He had run to Samuel, tucked in behind him, and was wrapped tightly around his father's leg.

"Hey little man do you want to join our *banda*?" asked the older boy, laughing. Saul said nothing, still hiding behind his Dad.

"Maybe you would like to become one of our *avioes* (little airplanes)," said another boy. They all laughed. Small children used by the gangs to deliver messages and drugs to their customers were called *avioes*.

A tall slender boy, who had been watching quietly in the background, now approached Samuel, moving closer and closer untill his face was only inches away from Samuel's. The boy, who the others addressed as *geral* (boss), appeared to be no more than 16 years of age, but his demeanor indicated that he was "the man." The man-boy was dressed in tight-legged levies and was wearing an expensive silk shirt, a thick braided gold chain around his neck, and was sporting $500, flame-red Giuseppe Zanotti sneakers.

He snarled at Samuel, "Give me your money, *babaca* (idiot)!" His eyes glared straight into Samuel's while his right hand slid down to rest on the butt of a pistol protruding from his untucked shirt above the waistband of his pants.

Samuel's mind raced. These boys were extremely dangerous and unpredictable. Samuel's mind raced, he had the safety of his little boy to think of— but there might be one thing that he could try.

He remembered an incident that had occurred months before with a mysterious man who he had encountered late one night near his home. Samuel had come across the man stranded in his very expensive luxury car. Samuel had repaired the car and had refused to accept any compensation. The grateful driver had insisted on repaying Samuel with some **very** confidential and valuable information.

Samuel, in the calmest voice that he could muster, responded to the now visibly agitated young *geral*. "I can give you what little money I have, but when my friends, the *brothers,* learn how I have been treated, it will be very bad for you."

"What brothers are these?" "You don't know any brothers."

"Of course *Geral*. You and I both know of the brothers of the Command, the PCC, Samuel replied.

"You know nothing of the PCC," the boy said, now sounding a bit unsure.

"I guess I will have to call my good friend *José*, You probably know of *José*, Samuel said, sounding impatient.

The obviously-rattled man-boy seemed suddenly impotent. He could not hide the terror that he was feeling at the consequences of angering this *José*. The boy had known of many associates that suddenly disappeared after angering a man of that name.

The g*eral* stepped back from Samuel, now attempting a sheepish smile. He said, "Please *senhor* (sir) ... I made a terrible mistake! Accept this gift and PLEASE do not speak of this to the *brothers*." Samuel did not respond but watched as the boys carefully placed the still intact watermelon back in the grocery bag and tossed in a wad of rolled bills.

As the gang hurriedly skulked away, Samuel took his son by the hand and reclaimed his grocery bag. The "man of questionable character" had shared some very privileged information—*his name*. It was to be used as a guarantee of protection in repayment for Samuel's act of kindness. The man had instructed Samuel in the dark secrets of criminal power in Sapopemba. The shadowy group, the Metropolitan First Command *(Primeiro Comando da Capital – PCC)*, controlled all criminal enterprises in the city, essentially even the judicial and police functions. The entire organization reported to one powerful individual. José, the stranded motorist that Samuel had assisted months before, was that man.

Brazil was not proving to offer the important fundamental benefits and opportunities that the family had hoped for: a safe and secure environment, religious tolerance, an honest government, and the potential to improve their lives.

Over the last decade, Brazilians had enjoyed steady gains in their standard of living but stagflation was now eroding those gains along with a 20% loss of the BRL value against the dollar. The country was also suffering a stunning government corruption scandal that involved the President's Workers Party, several prominent construction companies, and Petrobras, the nation's largest oil company. Brazil's current President Rousseff, who had previously been chairwoman of Petrobras, of course, denied any involvement or knowledge of the bribes taken in exchange for the lucrative contracts. Even the city's already poor infrastructure was becoming increasingly dysfunctional.[22]

Water availability could no longer be taken for granted due to a historic water drought. Some areas of the city still had reasonably good water delivery, but residents in higher locations like *Sapopemba*, which required more water pressure to reach them, were experiencing a water crisis. Residents had no choice but to buy water from the tanker trucks and avoid doing laundry or washing dishes.

For the sixth day in a row, Abigail found it necessary to trudge nearly 400 meters from the city's tanker truck to her home carrying a heavy four-gallon water jug. She had not been feeling well lately and the task of transporting water each day had become especially burdensome. Today on top of her fatigue she was also experiencing nausea.

There were plenty of factors to blame for the situation but no clear single villain. Changes in the weather patterns, deforestation, lack of government planning, and a soaring urban population were all obvious contributors. Whenever water service or rain water was available, people were doing all they could to store it in tubs, drums, buckets, or anything else that could contain it.

The standing water being collected and stored in such containers created the perfect environment for breeding mosquitos. As a result, the mosquito population had exploded and along with it came an outbreak of *dengue* fever. The potentially deadly disease had already infected more than 8,000 people in Sao Paulo with another 82,000 additional cases projected in the next few months. And now there was a mysterious new mosquito borne disease being reported, something called *zika virus*.[23]

At first, the Brazilian Health Ministry had showed little alarm as the virus symptoms appeared moderate and flu-like causing spots, itching, fever, headache, and muscle ache; however, there were recent studies that had pregnant women across the country in a panic. Scientists were now linking the virus to a rare incurable condition in infants, called *microcephaly*. These babies were born with abnormally small heads and suffered from brain damage with corresponding severe intellectual impairment, often leading to death. Officials had already reported 2,782 known cases with 40 deaths.[24]

Abigail, who was now five months along, was overjoyed that God had gifted them with a miraculous second pregnancy. But this recent news, regarding the *zika* virus, had created in her an even higher state of anxiety. The couple's hopes of creating a better, safer life in this new country were quickly fading.

Chapter 7

The Last Straw

It was 8:30 p.m. and the 16-year-old boy was on his way to deliver his 14th *Pizzaria Florenza* pizza of the evening and, hopefully, his last. This part of Osasco was known to be dangerous, and he was not comfortable being in this area after dark.

His mother allowed him to use her treasured car in the evenings so he could earn some money of his own. If he hurried with the delivery, he would have time to stop and see his girlfriend and still make it home by his 10 p.m. curfew.

Finding no open parking, he double-parked outside of the *Bar do Ciduca,* a popular bar in this district of Osasco. He would quickly run the pizza inside, receive payment—with *hopefully* a substantial tip—and get back to the car before the police could issue a parking ticket. The boy hurried into the darkened bar and spotted the group of young men who had likely placed the order. They had the look and dress of local mafia gang members, but in spite of their unsavory status, such shady characters had given him exceptionally generous tips in the past.

"*Homenzinho* (little man), over here!" ordered one of the group's older appearing members, maybe in his early 20's. As the boy hurried across the dimly lit bar, he stumbled over the outstretched leg of a seated patron, nearly dropping the extra-large "works" pizza.

"I'm so sorry," the boy apologized.

"*Babaca* (stupid person!)" shouted the man. The drunken man had risen from his stool and now stood, menacingly, blocking the boy's path.

"*Ô, meu. Que é isso* (What's your problem, dude?)" asked the boy.

"Leave the boy alone!" snarled the older gang member, "he has bigger culhões (testicles) than you do!" Muttering to himself, the man meekly sat down, allowing the boy to pass.

Having received payment and a very nice tip from the gang's leader, the boy turned and started for the exit. He was anxious to move his double-parked car and hurry over to his girlfriend Gabriela's house.

Just before he reached the door, he heard the screeching of tires and slamming car doors outside. It was probably the police—he would get a ticket now for sure!

With a loud crash, the heavy wooden entry door exploded open. Even in the dim lighting, he could see a glint of light reflecting from the assault rifle's steel barrel. The first man rushed in, knocking the boy to the floor, and was quickly followed by five more armed men, all dressed in dark clothing and wearing women's black nylon stockings over their faces and heads.

Two of the men yanked the young boy from the floor, pushed him back into the bar, and directed him to join the startled gang members in the back, who had just begun to devour their pizza.

Ignoring other bar patrons, the masked intruders seemed interested only in the frightened gang members and now had their weapons pointed, menacingly, at their heads.

The man who had been first through the door seemed to be in charge.

Were these men robbers or police? They had no uniforms but operated like police.

"Every one of you *putas, filho da* (sons of a whore), tell me your names and if you have criminal records. Don't lie to me, or I promise—it won't go well for you!" the man in charge bellowed.

One by one, the gang members stated their names, some confessing to have criminal records.

The terrified pizza delivery boy, who had never been in any trouble, nervously stated his name and declared his clean record, thinking, "surely it must be obvious that he was not one of the gang members."

"You *cucharachas* (cockroaches) are all filthy liars," the leader said calmly. "Do you want to know what my men do to lying cockroaches?"

Abigail was worried. She and Samuel both had work today, and Saul's always dependable sitter, Guelo, his "big brother," was extremely late. She had dialed Ama's number several times already to inquire about her son, but she had gotten a busy signal each time. Where was Guelo?

This time she heard the phone ringing, finally—she should have left for work 20 minutes ago.

At the very first ring, Ama picked up. "Guelo, Guelo," she inquired in a frantic voice.

"No Ama, its Abigail, I was expecting Guelo. He had promised to sit with Saul today—he should have been here some time ago!

"Oh Abi, Guelo never came home from work last night—he should have been home at least by 10 p.m. His girlfriend hasn't seen him and none of his friends have heard from him. I've called every hospital and just now called the police. Abi, I'm terrified! This is not like him at all."

It was later that morning when Abigail, who had canceled her work shift to stay with her son, heard back from Ama.

"He's gone Abi! Guelo, my boy is dead!" she wailed.

"What! What do you mean, he's dead?" responded Abigail, dumbfounded.

"He is dead; murdered while making a delivery—no reason why—ten boys slaughtered. Why, why my son?" sobbed the distraught mother.

Abigail heard the phone go dead as Ama, now moaning uncontrollably, was unable to continue. Abigail hung up the phone and collapsed on the floor in tears.

For the next several days, Sao Paulo news was full of reports that speculated on the violence. Authorities were investigating the possibility that these were targeted killings of drug traffickers and criminals. There had actually been a total of five separate attacks with a total of 18 young men executed. Three separate attacks had taken place in Osasco and two more nearby in the district of Barueri. Many people believed that the murders were committed by off duty police officers in retaliation for the recent killings of two officers. The department head of public safety would say only that, "The involvement of police officers in the case was one of the theories under consideration."[25]

In Brazil, with one of the highest murder rates (53,000 in 2013) in the world, 11,197 of those *(officially reported)* were killed by police officers.[26]

It was especially alarming that the majority of these massacres of "troublesome individuals" targeted young black men, *Pretas*. The shocking statistics clearly pointed to a racially motivated component in the executions.

Samuel and Abigail had fled Africa because of war, but here there was also war. This war was being waged, above the law, by Sao Paulo police officers on targeted factions of their own discretion.

The family had been in Brazil for almost a year now and were struggling to exist on their low paying incomes. They had become increasingly fearful of the escalating violence and, now with Abigail's pregnancy, they were faced with the new threat posed by the rapidly-spreading *zika* virus—it seems that the *"shadow of death"* had followed them from Africa.

The awful gut-wrenching reality of Guelo's murder, had galvanized their decision. The family would leave their home once again and, hopefully, reach the promised land of America or Canada.

While serving at Biyou' Z, Abigail often overheard the conversations that were taking place over coffee or a meal. Often the stories were of friends or relatives who had attempted to gain asylum in the United States or Canada. Many had taken the arduous and extremely dangerous route across Brazil and then traveled north along the *"Migrant Trail"* through the entirety of South America and the length of Mexico.

The journey required walking hundreds of miles through the jungle, paying bribes to smugglers, corrupt police and judicial officials, all while risking becoming victims of robbery by ever-present thieves.

Some had given up along the way, most had been arrested, and many had died making the attempt. Of those who were successful in completing the long trek, less than 30% had been granted asylum after reaching the U.S.

The journey through this corridor had been attempted by migrants from all over the world, all hoping to find safety and security in North America. In addition to the typical migrants from South American and Mexico, there had been an increasing influx from Bangladesh, Nepal, China, India, Pakistan, Tibet, Cuba, Cameroon, Somalia, Eritrea, Ghana, Sudan, Angola, and Nigeria.[27] As many as 3,000 Africans had attempted the journey in the past year alone.

Everyone that had learned of the family's intention discouraged them from attempting the journey—especially with Abigail's pregnant condition.

Samuel and Abigail wrestled over the decision. They knew that they could not obtain travel visas to America so instead attempted to obtain visas to Canada where Abigail's disabled sister was located. Her sister had offered to take them in, but that application was also rejected.

The family could travel by air as far as Costa Rica, which did not require a visa, but that would be very expensive.

Samuel had wisely preserved money from the sale of his business and truck when leaving Angola and was prepared for a need such as this. His major concern was Abigail. She was more than five months pregnant and would be putting herself and the unborn baby at risk in attempting the difficult and strenuous trip.

"Samuel, you should go on ahead with Saul. You can carry him on your back and he can walk some of the time. I will stay here until the baby is born and we will follow you in a few months," suggested Abigail.

"Abi, there is no way that I'm going to leave you here alone!" he replied. "That is not an option, I will not leave my wife and baby behind."

Abigail said nothing for a minute as she considered Samuel's resolve, then spoke. "Samuel, I am a strong woman. I can make the journey. We can make it together. God will be with us, as he has always been. We will trust in him."

"Abi, I trust in God too but even God will think this is a foolish idea."

"No Samuel, I *know* that he will guard and protect us just as he promises in Psalms 23:

"The Lord is my shepherd;
 I shall not want.
He makes me to lie down in green pastures;
He leads me beside the still waters.
He restores my soul;

He leads me in paths of righteousness for his name's sake.
*Yea, though I walk through **the valley of the shadow of death, I will fear no evil;***
For you are with me;
Your rod and your staff, they comfort me.
You prepare a table before me in the presence of my enemies;
You anoint my head with oil;
My cup runs over.
Surely goodness and mercy shall follow me
All the days of my life;
And I will dwell in the house of the Lord forever."

Samuel sat there quietly looking at Abigail's face. He knew this face so well— this was the face of a woman who could not be swayed. He would soon be leading his little boy and very pregnant wife on the journey of their lives.

"OK Abi, we will all go together."

Chapter 8

Costa Rica

Within a month, the family had prepared to leave Sao Paulo. They had said their goodbyes to Melinito, Ama, and all their other close friends. They would particularly miss those two women who had been such a great blessing to them while living in Brazil. The few household items they owned had been sold or given away and they had pared down their clothing, essential belongings, and personal documents to fit inside three bags.

They would fly four hours from Sao Paulo to Lima Peru aboard Avianca Airlines flight 6646, the national airline of Colombia and change flights at *Aeropuerto Internacional Jorge Chávez*, Peru's primary airport. After a two-hour layover in Lima, they would board Avianca flight 624 on to San Jose's *Juan Santamaria* airport in Costa Rica, landing there at 1:50 p.m.

Having flown once before, both Samuel and Saul were a little less anxious during this trip. The shorter travel time was also much less grueling than the long trip from Turkey to Sao Paulo had been eight months earlier.

They touched down at *Juan Santamaria* airport at 2:15 p.m. and deplaned with only their carry-on bags and their son. Samuel had planned the trip as far as the Costa Rican border but not much beyond. After they crossed over the border into Nicaragua, the plan would have to evolve one day, one situation at a time.

With the family's 90-day visitation permits and required Yellow Fever vaccination papers in order, processing through immigration was uneventful.

Samuel inquired at the Airport's transportation counter and made bus reservations for the trip to *Liberia* about 300 km north. The city of *Liberia* was still about an hour from the Nicaraguan border near the city of *La Cruz* but offered hotel rooms that were much less expensive that those located nearer the border. Samuel secured the family a room there for $30 a night.

By 4 p.m. they were on the *Pulmitan de Liberia* bus and headed for the day's final destination. They had been traveling now for 15 hours and were all very weary.

The sleek blue, yellow, and white double-deck bus provided comfortable seats and air-conditioning. This bus ride would offer the final comfortable transport the family would experience over the next few months. The family was too tired to enjoy the spectacular scenery which was gliding by outside the bus's large tinted windows, but the three hungry travelers did find the energy to consume some water and snacks which Abigail had purchased before leaving the bus station.

Samuel finally closed his eyes, allowing his head to fall back against the headrest, and sat wondering what unknown challenges might be lying ahead for the family. Then with Saul tucked under his arm he slept, oblivious to the droning diesel engine behind him, for the remainder of the five hour trip.

The interior lights were switched on as the driver guided the huge bus into the brightly illuminated Liberia station. Abigail awakened Saul and they gathered their things to leave. It was just after 9 p.m. as they stepped off the bus. While Abigail and Saul took a bathroom break, Samuel inquired about directions to their hotel.

The hotel was about 8 km south on Inter American Highway 1, and beyond walking distance, so the family would need to find a taxi.

Hospedaje Guanasol was a typical looking two-story building, similar to budget motels found in every country of the world. In the illumination of the lone mercury vapor street light, the building's salmon color stucco appeared more a sickly gray-green. Just outside the walkway overhangs were clusters of small palm trees—a modest attempt at landscaping.

The taxi drove across the large dirt and gravel parking lot to the illuminated office which had its entry door and windows covered with steel bars, as did the entire building.

The majority of guests staying at *Hospedaje Guanasol* were there to visit the nearby *Africa Safari Costa Rica* animal park. Samuel found it ironic that his (African) family would now find themselves far from home in Costa Rica near a tourist park that had been created solely to offer visitors a small taste of Africa. After paying the $30 per night fee, the exhausted family checked into their first floor room, number 107, where they would find a double bed for him and Abigail, a single bed for Saul, and small TV, all crammed into a tiny 108 square foot space. Minimal as it was, this room would be remembered as their last true luxury accommodation.

First thing the following morning, Samuel spoke with the hotel clerk who recommended a small internet equipped coffee shop nearby where the family could get breakfast and perhaps find someone who would be knowledgeable about crossing the border into Nicaragua. Samuel was obviously not the first guest to make such an inquiry.

Samuel planned for the family to submit themselves to immigration authorities at the Nicaraguan border crossing at *Peñas Blancas*. They would present their African passports, declare their intention to seek political asylum in the U.S. or Canada, and request a temporary visa for passage through the country.

As Abigail and Saul sat in the coffee shop having breakfast, Samuel sat nearby chatting with another black skinned man, apparently a local. Although the man spoke Spanish, the primary language of Costa Rica, Samuel's Portuguese was similar enough to allow for a decent conversation.

What he learned from the man was alarming. The border had recently been ordered **closed** to all migrant traffic! The man explained that the closure had resulted from a domino effect of closures which moved from north to south beginning with Nicaragua.

In a desperate effort to stem a dramatic increase in the flow of migrants, Nicaragua had closed its border with Costa Rica. In addition to the more normal numbers of Haitians, Africans, and Pakistanis, there had been a huge recent influx of Cubans. Following Nicaragua's decision, Costa Rica closed its border with Panama and then Panama closed its border with Colombia.

No one knew when the borders would reopen. It was expected to be soon, but it seemed unlikely that the family would be traveling north—at least not for several more days.

Eight days had passed and still no movement at the border. This had never happened before and no one seemed to know if, or when, the border would be reopened. As he waited, Samuel occupied his days by alternating his time with Abigail and Saul at the hotel and hanging out at the coffee shop. He had quickly become friends with the shop owner and several regular customers. His new friends allowed him to check the most current border status using their internet linked cell phones.

One of the regulars informed Samuel about a group of African migrants that were reported to be renting an old vacant warehouse on the outskirts of Liberia while they also waited to cross the border. Samuel decided to find the group in the hope that they might know some additional information regarding the border closure. He could not have too many friends, or new information, in such a critical situation.

Samuel was able to hitch a ride into Liberia that dropped him off within a 15-minute-walking distance from the warehouse. Having heard the sound of voices as he approached, he knew that the rusty old structure was occupied.

Each of the industrial building's large doors were rolled up in order to encourage ventilation, since the corrugated-metal construction had neither insulation nor air-conditioning.

Samuel knocked on the thin metal wall near the open door calling out, "Hello there."

"Welcome my friend," answered a voice inside. The language was English but spoken with a distinctive Tigrinya accent which Samuel recognized as Eritrean. "Please come in."

Samuel entered the stiflingly hot interior and introduced himself to his hosts. "I am Samuel from Nigeria, and I am traveling north with my Angolan wife and baby. We have come by way of Brazil."

"My name is Kifle, and this is my friend Nebay. We are coming from the area of Adi Quala in Eritrea near the Ethiopian border. We have been staying here for 12 days now with 15 other people from Somolia, Ghana, and Kenya, all men, except one pregnant woman. We are all stuck in this place waiting for the border to be opened again."

Kifle offered Samuel a bottle of water and invited him to sit down in one of the vacant plastic chairs—the only furniture in the building. The men had purchased two small fans which were directed toward the chairs but, even working at maximum speed, they had little impact on the air temperature.

After chatting for a while and sharing the scant information that they had regarding the border closure, Kifle began to tell Samuel of the trials that he and his friend Nebay had survived just to reach Costa Rica.[28]

The two friends had embarked on the grueling journey from Eritrea motivated by the same desires that fueled most refugees to seek refuge from the violence in their home countries and the opportunity to live a more prosperous life in America. Their route had taken them first to Turkey, and then on to Brazil, just as Samuel and Abigail had traveled earlier, then they continued across the continent to Ecuador taking advantage of its visa free immigration policy. From there they had crossed illegally into Colombia by offering the border guards a $100 bribe.

Kifle continued, "In Columbia we met a smuggler named Carlos. He promised that he could get us across the border to Panama for $450 each. The trip took us three full days. Each day we hiked many grueling miles through hot, dense, bush terrain and at night we traveled along the rocky coastline on leaky wooden *pangas*, which are flimsy outboard-motor powered fishing boats.

We were terrified for the entire trip since there are many robbers that look for migrants to beat, rob, and sometimes kill. We were arrested almost immediately after crossing into Panama and were put into a detention facility where we stayed for several weeks—at least they fed us there. Finally, we were put onto a bus and deported back to a Colombian refugee center."

"So how did you finally make it through Panama and reach this place?" Samuel asked.

"After we were released and issued short-term travel visas, we traveled to the city of Turbo on the Caribbean coast hoping to travel by sea around the isthmus of Capaburga to La Meil in Panama. Smugglers there demanded $750 each for the trip and we could not pay that much. We had used up most of our money paying bribes to border authorities, so we had no choice but to try crossing into Panama through the jungle. We found an agent (smuggler) that would take us and these five other men from Ghana by canoe down the *Cacarica'* river to the edge of the jungle, the beginning of the *Darian Gap*."

The area surrounding Turbo had become a bottleneck for migrant traffic north due to the difficulty of crossing into Costa Rica. The 19,000 mile Pan American Highway connects all of the Americas from Buenos Aires in Argentina to Prudhoe Bay at the northern edge of Alaska, **except** the 40-mile jungle stretch known as the *Darian Gap*. No travel option by road exists at all. Those that had the money could attempt the faster passage by sea but even that method had proven extremely dangerous. Traveling the rough seas by night in a jam-packed skiff without life jackets was frightening enough, but migrants also ran the risk of encountering paramilitary groups or drug trafficking gangs that controlled the corridor. The notorious *clan Usaga* (drug gang) actively utilized this sea route and had been blamed in the recent robbing and drowning of 20 migrants only two weeks earlier.

Migrants who could not afford to travel by boat were left with only one choice–trekking through the inhospitable jungle of the *Darian Gap*. Smuggling fees for this option were much cheaper, with costs ranging from $200-$500 dollars, but the jungle route was even more dangerous than the sea route.

"I have heard many horrible stories of people who died while crossing through that jungle. I'm amazed that you both survived," Samuel marveled.

"It is one of the hottest and wettest places on the planet," Kifle stated flatly. "Besides the dangers from animals, we had to avoid Los *Urabeños* (drug runners) that operate along the eastern neck of the isthmus as well as members of the rebel group, *FARC*."

The 57th Front of the Revolutionary Armed Forces of Colombia (*FARC*), who called the jungle home, demanded a cut from any smuggler who wanted safe passage through any area of their control.

"Once we left the *Cacarica*' river, we trekked for days through viper-infested, hot, steaming, thick jungle. During the day there was no way to cool off and mosquitos, some that carry malaria, tormented us constantly. At night there were blood-sucking bats and jaguars that kept us from sleeping. We threw away everything that we were carrying except water and our important documents. After six days we finally ran out of water. We were then forced to drink the muddy polluted jungle river water. Most of us got skin boils and diarrhea which made us extremely weak."

Samuel could only shake his head in disbelief as he processed the story that he was hearing.

"My friend John", Kifle continued, motioning to the slight man seated across from Samuel, "became so weak that he collapsed. We tried to push him to move on but he refused—he could not go on. We had no choice but to leave him."

Kifle's mood turned solemn as he continued, "we saw a lot of dead in the jungle, lots of decomposing bodies and skeletons. We had gashes all over from the sharp leaves and were covered in insect bites. We all believed that we would die there in the jungle. We had been without food for four days. Finally, after eight days in the jungle, we stumbled out at the small village of *Paya* where we found refuge."

"Thanks be to God that a Panamanian Police patrol came across John alive that same day, and brought him to *Paya* as well, where he was able to recover. We turned ourselves into authorities at *Meteti*, who took our fingerprints and checked for criminal history. We were kept in detention there for 25 days and received two meals each day, which consisted only of rice. When we were finally cleared we were given temporary permits that allowed us legal passage through Panama. Now here we are, still waiting to have the border open, and hopefully Nicaraguan authorities will give us papers to continue our journey."

"Wow," Samuel exclaimed, "You have all shown such incredible courage just to come this far. You are very brave!"

"Or perhaps stupid," Nebay, who had said nothing, volunteered. They all laughed in agreement.

After hearing their story, Samuel was even more grateful that he and Abi had been able to travel by plane from Brazil to Costa Rica. He was not so sure that in similar conditions he would have had the same commitment and resolve that had been demonstrated by this group of people. What unknown struggles and hardships would his own family face over the rest of their journey?

Samuel exchanged contact information with Kifle and promised to share any announcement in regards to the reopening of the border. After hugging each of his new friends and wishing them "Godspeed," he began his walk back to the highway hoping to hitch a ride back home to the hotel.

Chapter 9

Nicaragua

It was coming up on three weeks since the family had arrived in Costa Rica, and there was still no indication of when the border might be opened. The cost of the extended hotel stay was draining the family's remaining resources. With each day that passed, the couple was becoming increasingly concerned that Abigail, now entering her seventh month of pregnancy, would not be able to continue the strenuous trip north.

They had reached a critical decision point. Either they would need to stay put in Costa Rica and allow Abi to give birth there before moving on or run the physical risks of traveling with her highly compromised condition.

"Abi, we can't wait any longer. Either I will need to find work, maybe in the car wash, and we will have the baby here, or we must find someone to help us cross the border. We have no idea when the border will reopen or if it will be reopened at all!"

"Samuel, I don't want to give birth here or stay here any longer. I can still walk so we will go. We can find another way."

"I think it's too dangerous for you Abi, we could lose the baby."

"God will continue to protect us Samuel, he always has!" she declared. "I can make it!"

Two days later, Samuel was introduced to a woman at the internet cafe. This woman, Carmen, was a Nicaraguan citizen and was known to *assist* (smuggle) people illegally over the border. Carmen was young, perhaps in her late 20's, but seemed quite competent and businesslike. She was short, barely five feet tall, with a slender frame and fit body. She wore her long hair pulled back in a ponytail which protruded through the opening of a black baseball cap.

"I can get you across for $500," she told Samuel.

"That seems like too much money for a one day crossing," he argued.

"Remember, I normally charge $200 each—so $500 for three people is very cheap."

Samuel quickly realized that there would be no child discount for this kind of service.

He considered for a moment, then answered, "OK, we will do it. How soon can we leave?"

"I am concerned about your pregnant wife—this is not an easy trip," Carmen stated.

"My wife is a very strong woman Carmen, and she is determined to do this!"

"We will leave by bus early tomorrow afternoon and travel to a small town called *Sonzapote* between the city of *La Cruz* and the Peñas *Blancas* border crossing. From there we will travel at night on foot using the mountain route to avoid the border police on both sides," Carmen instructed.

At 5 p.m. the following day, Samuel and his family arrived at the Liberia bus station and purchased tickets for the ride north. Carmen arrived soon after and purchased her ticket but did not acknowledge the family, as she had made clear in their previous meeting.

Samuel had already paid her fee and had transferred the family's identification documents and birth certificates to her for safe keeping in her backpack. In the event that they were stopped by police along the way, the family would claim that they were Nicaraguan citizens who happened to be traveling without identification.

The one-hour ride north on this local bus was far different from the experience they had enjoyed on the plush bus ride from San José three weeks earlier. This vehicle was old and battered from years of punishment on the rough dirt and gravel roads which were typical near the border. Even at this late afternoon hour, the temperature inside was soaring, and the bus's vintage AC was no match for the soaking heat from the relentless sun outside.

The family did not sit near Carmen during the trip but followed her off when she got up to exit at an obscure stop just east of *La Cruz*.

The only signs of civilization to be seen at the stop were three buildings—a small market, a two-pump gas station, and a tiny post office.

Samuel and Abi followed behind Carmen as she entered the market. Carmen spoke to Samuel briefly, only to advise him that they purchase as much water as they could carry. The water would be heavy but an absolute life-necessity in order for them to complete the trek.

Samuel bought 7.5 liters (2 gallons) of bottled water. Already conscious of the 16-pound weight, he wondered how the next 12-hour adventure would unfold.

As Samuel paid for the water, the clerk nodded wishing the four travelers, "Good Luck." Obviously, he was aware of what the group was about to attempt—he had seen visitors with similar intentions pass through his store before.

For the next half-hour Carmen led them along the edge of the dirt road. They had encountered no automobile traffic so far, but they remained wary that in this open terrain they could quickly be spotted by suspicious police patrols who might come along.

They had walked about a half-mile when Carmen abruptly turned off the road at a subtle break in the undergrowth. The trail opening was so obscure that Samuel would not have recognized it as such. The narrow path was surrounded by tall brush and appeared to be quickly rising in elevation. It was already dusk. Samuel knew that they would soon be walking in darkness but, hopefully, the clear evening would provide the hikers some light from the stars.

Carmen led the procession, followed by Abigail, then little Saul with Samuel bringing up the rear. The family was very fit and they were quite used to walking since they had been without a car for nearly a year in Brazil. Saul was enjoying the trek so far, seeing it as a great adventure, and happy to be free of his three-week confinement to the hotel grounds. Abigail frequently had to "shush" the boy as he was having a difficult time staying quiet. It was imperative that they make as little noise as possible since they did not want to alert a roving police patrol or, worse, robbers that commonly preyed on lone individuals or small groups of migrants. Abi told Saul that they were playing a "quiet" game and that he would win a prize if he did not make a sound—that seemed to be working for now.

It was completely dark now. Carmen carried a flashlight which she turned on occasionally, but for only a brief moment in order to establish the trail's direction. The party had been hiking for almost two hours now and

Abigail desperately needed to stop and rest. They all needed water and drank from the jug that Abi was carrying in order to lighten her load.

After a brief rest the group continued on, speaking only when absolutely necessary. The only sounds made were from the unavoidable cracking of twigs underfoot and the labored breathing of the four hikers. Occasionally they could hear calls from some of the bush animals, tapirs, anteaters, birds of every variety, and poisonous frogs. Nicaragua had the greatest forested area of any South American country and was home to over 1,400 animal species including the, frequently encountered, Mantled Howler monkey. These large monkeys were capable of the loudest call of any land animal, and they were quick to vocalize when agitated or threatened. The hikers weren't particularly concerned about the monkeys but definitely hoped to avoid one of the fiercest predators on the planet, the jaguar, one of several large cat species common to the country.

The uneven ground and multitude of exposed tree roots crossing the trail caused frequent stumbling for the four hikers. As a result, their progress was agonizingly slow. Often there appeared to be no trail at all. It was no wonder that many of the individuals who had attempted to make this trip without a guide had become hopelessly lost for days— some had even died.

Scattered openings in the canopy of tall dense vegetation allowed scant starlight to reach the ground.

Since the hikers were traveling without flashlights in order to minimize the likelihood of apprehension, the lack of illumination made the walking even more treacherous. Abigail had fallen twice so far, but Samuel had been able to catch her and prevent serious injury.

Carmen was certain that they had crossed the border within the past hour, but of course there were no markers to delineate the actual boundary. If they had been in cell phone range Carmen's phone mapping function could have been used to determine their precise location.

It was becoming necessary to stop more frequently now as both Abigail and Saul were extremely fatigued. The tiny boy had to walk faster than the adults in order for his little legs to cover the same ground. Abigail was also struggling—carrying the additional weight of her unborn baby was taking a huge toll.

Eventually they broke out of the forest and into a small clearing where Carmen announced that they would make an extended rest stop. Samuel had been carrying Saul on his back, as well as their belongings for the past hour, and was now just as fatigued as Abigail.

It was around 2 a.m. and the four hadn't eaten anything for the past 14 hours, so they were extremely hungry. Abi had packed a bag of pretzels and a box of raisins which they shared between gulps of precious water. The salty pretzels would help them to retain water and prevent dehydration—that could become a problem since they had very little water left in their jugs.

The four exhausted hikers collapsed on the ground and made themselves as comfortable as the inhospitable conditions allowed. Abi and Samuel leaned back against a large tree and laid their tired little boy across his daddy's lap. After torturous hours of walking, it felt wonderful for them to drop their packs and to get off of their feet, especially for Abi.

The clearing in the canopy allowed an unobstructed view of the heavens. With the absence of any artificial light source, the starry sky's brightness was extraordinarily spectacular. Samuel thought it ironic that they could be in this idyllic setting of remarkable beauty while engaged in such a strenuous and life-threatening challenge. If it weren't for the constant annoyance of buzzing mosquitos, the scene could have been quite pleasant.

Up to this time Samuel had never engaged in any personal discussion with their guide Carmen. Every prior conversation had been strictly business.

"Have you made this trip many times before?" Samuel inquired.

"Oh yes—many, many times," Carmen replied. "I have been helping people to cross into Nicaragua for more than three years. It has been the only means of supporting my son and myself."

"So you also have a son?"

"Yes, my little *Juanito* is four years old—just a little older than Saul. I have been a single mother since he was born. His father left us as when I became pregnant. It has been a very hard life!"

"Have you ever been caught by the border police?" Samuel asked.

"Two times. The first time they kept me in jail for three weeks. They finally released me after I agreed to pay them a bribe. The second time, the officer asked for a bribe immediately—$300. I paid and we all went on our way. You can never be sure what they will do. It is a hard business. Unfortunately, these bribes are just a cost of doing business."

"It's a tough way to make a living," Samuel replied.

Abigail, totally exhausted, had been asleep for the entire time with her head resting on Samuel's shoulder, and Saul hadn't moved since first falling asleep across his lap.

It was hard to believe that a full hour had passed when Carmen roused the family. "We should go now," she said softly as she stood and shouldered her backpack.

The family gathered their things and fell back into order, once again following Carmen back into the dense forest. The terrain became flatter as they crested the mountain—a welcome change after hours of rising elevation.

Samuel again carried Saul on his back. The falling elevation made climbing less strenuous, but even so, Abigail was struggling. She had to be extra cautious as the downhill slope didn't favor her pregnant body's center of gravity, and the physical discomfort of her swollen abdomen made every movement doubly hard. Eventually, the gently-descending trail would drop into a valley that would take them out of the dense undergrowth and on to their destination.

Carmen stopped them once again to caution that maintaining silence from this point on was imperative. During the final two hours of this trek, the risk of encountering either robbers or police patrols would increase dramatically.

It was still dark, about 4:30 a.m. when Carmen halted them abruptly, "Hush!" she whispered.

Waving her outstretched hand, she motioned them off the path and back into the thick undergrowth. They crouched there in the darkness, hearts beating wildly and unsure of just what danger had prompted Carmen to send them into hiding. Then perhaps 100 meters down the trail they caught a glimpse of the moving light that had put Carmen on alert. The light appeared to flicker as it became visible through intermittent openings in the thick vegetation but, without a doubt, whoever carried it was moving quickly toward them.

Little Saul, who had been asleep in Samuel's arms, was beginning to wake and quietly murmur. Samuel tightened his grip on the boy's arm and whispered in his ear, "be very quiet son, we are playing *hide and seek,* you must not make a sound!"

The groggy boy did not seem to comprehend, but thankfully, he fell back to sleep.

They crouched there motionless, hearts pounding, as three men armed with assault rifles shuffled by less than five meters away. As they passed by Carmen could tell from the few words that she overheard that these men were not police—they were robbers.

The four frightened hikers remained concealed and motionless for at least five more minutes until they were absolutely certain that the threat had passed. When the flickering light and muffled voices had faded back into the darkness, Carmen motioned the family out of hiding and back onto the narrow trail. She and her clients had been extremely fortunate—this time.

Chapter 10

Caught in the Net

As they walked the last half-mile down to the valley floor, it was just beginning to become light. Soon the party would be reaching an area that was considered to be safe.

The miles of thick brush and jagged tree roots tearing at her flesh had left Abigail's arms and legs lacerated and bleeding. She was wearing only a thin fabric sarong since her pregnant body made the wearing of pants impossible. Through all the affliction, she had never complained or considered stopping. Samuel knew that she had been in pain for most of the journey, but he was not at all surprised by her stoic resolve—he was so proud of his wife.

The party had been walking for over nine hours and had covered about 11 miles of the difficult serpentine trail. If they could have walked "as the crow flies," the hike would have been only a three-mile trek, but using the long winding mountain route was the only way that they could, hopefully, avoid the authorities.

In a mile or so they would break out of the undergrowth and onto a dirt road. The lightly traveled road provided the only vehicle-accessible connection between sparsely populated villages in the area. There, within a mile of the small village of *Pueblo Nuevo*, the family hoped to disappear into the local population and continue their way north across the country.

Suddenly the stillness was interrupted by a chorus of earsplitting cries! The party had startled a band of Howler monkeys who were now erupting in deafening cries of alarm. This was a very bad thing! The monkeys' call could be heard for up to 10 miles and would certainly alert any police patrol nearby that someone was passing through the area.

Fewer than 10 minutes had passed when, just as Carmen feared, four police officers materialized out of the bush around the party, two in front of them and two at their rear.

Anticipating just such a possibility, Carmen had increased the distance between herself and the family so that they might appear to be traveling separately. She was carrying the family's Angolan passports in her own backpack so that, if apprehended, the family could claim that they were Nicaraguans.

"Alto, Alto!" shouted the officer who had stepped out in front of Carmen. His face looked surprisingly youthful, as if he had not yet shaved, and he was certainly no older than 20 years of age. The young man wore the familiar uniform of the Nicaraguan police, dark blue loose-fitting pants which were bloused into black military-style boots, and a light blue shirt. The shirt had a single white stripe on each dark blue shoulder epilate which, Carmen had learned, signified some rank. Rank or no rank, Carmen knew that the young officer had to be inexperienced—that could work in her favor.

"¿Cuál es el problema (what's the problem)?" Carmen asked politely.

"Déjame ver tu identificación (let me see your identification)," he ordered.

Carmen took off her backpack, pulled her Nicaraguan driver's license out, and calmly presented it to the young officer.

"Where are you going?" he asked.

"I am on my way to visit my sister who lives nearby in *Pueblo Nuevo*."

"And who are these people?" he inquired, gesturing toward the family as they approached from behind and followed closely by the other two officers,

"I don't know them—I was not aware that they were behind me," she said, attempting to appear surprised.

Apparently satisfied with Carmen's explanation, the officer returned her license and waved her on, his attention now fixed on the three family members being escorted toward him.

"Let me see your papers!" he barked.

Samuel, in the best Spanish that he could muster, attempted a response, "We are not carrying any identification. We did not expect to need it. Our car has broken down so we are walking to *Quebrada Arriba* from our home in *Condega*." Carmen had prepped him beforehand with this explanation in the event that they were apprehended by the police

"You don't sound Nicaraguan—your Spanish is poor," quipped the skeptical officer.

"We speak mostly English in our family," Samuel stated, now speaking English. "My father's family came here from Africa many years ago and we have always spoken English."

"Your Spanish sounds more like Portuguese to my ears," snickered their interrogator. "We must arrest you and take you back to our station in order to sort out your citizenship."

"Unless *perhaps*," the officer slowly removed his baseball style cap and held it open in front of Samuel while, at the same time, rubbing his thumb and middle finger together—unmistakable indications that the he was proposing a bribe in exchange for their release.

"I could offer you $100 if you will let us go," Samuel responded—clearly understanding the gestures.

The four officers snickered heartily at hearing Samuel's *pitiful* offer, obviously amused at the leverage they held.

$500—no less than $500," demanded the officer in charge.

Samuel lifted his shirt to expose a money belt, which he proceeded to unzip, and carefully withdrew its contents. He held out $300 to the officer, pleading, "This is the last of our money. Please take it and let us go. You will not see us again."

The men, now considering the $300, shrugged their shoulders in kind of a "*whatever*" sign of agreement.

As the lead officer plucked the money from Samuel's money belt, he warned the family one last time, "If we ever see you again or we won't be so easy on you!"

Before the family had even disappeared down the trail the four corrupt police officers had already begun to divide their ill-gotten spoils.

Carmen had been waiting out of sight about 100 meters down the trail and rejoined the family as they approached.

"You are lucky that they let you go for only $300," she remarked. "These young police officers tend to be most ruthless and greedy!"

Samuel was not feeling lucky, but he was extremely grateful that the bulk of the family's savings, which had been hidden inside his spare socks, had not been discovered when the officers searched their backpacks.

The family was shaken from the frightening encounter with the police, but they were excited that the remaining walk to the village of *Pueblo Nuevo* and relative safety, was not far.

The sprawling valley's vegetation was much less dense than they had experienced at the higher elevations, and the group found the walking much easier. The narrow path had finally intersected a dirt road that ran between remote villages in the area. The road's damp earth showed clear tire imprints left by recent traffic. The party would need to stay alert for the sounds of approaching vehicles in order to have ample time to get off the road and hide.

Feeling that most of the danger was behind them, the group was in good spirits and were beginning to believe that they were finally safe. As the family followed their guide along the dirt road, Samuel began considering what they would do after parting ways with Carmen at *Pueblo Nuevo*, their contracted destination.

50 meters ahead, the road had been cut away by torrents of water from one of the region's frequent monsoonal rains, leaving them no option other than to wade across the fast moving river.

The three adults removed their shoes and began wading through the murky brown water. Carmen led, followed by Abigail and Samuel, with Saul on his father's back. They worked their way carefully around a bend in the road, keeping to the shallower side which paralleled a rocky bluff.

Carmen was the first to step around the bend when she stopped abruptly, stunned to see yet another police patrol. It was too late to hide as the police patrol, who were just as surprised as Carmen, had already spotted them.

This patrol consisted of three police officers. One, who was in the process of lighting a cigar, was sitting in the cab of a mud-spattered, blue on blue 4WD Toyota crew cab which was parked alongside the road. The insignia on the shoulder patches of his uniform carried both a stripe and a diamond design so, presumably, he was the higher ranking officer.

The other officers, one man and one woman, had no insignia at all. These two officers were sitting on mud covered Honda ATV's, which had surely been the vehicles that had left the distinctive tracks in the road.

The ranking officer quickly ordered his subordinates to gather up the suspicious barefoot hikers. After allowing them to put on their shoes, the two officers paraded the unlucky party over to their superior. The senior officer had remained in the truck, sitting with one leg out of the open door, casually puffing on his cigar. Printed on the nameplate below his badge was the name R. Diaz.

Appearing to be around 50 years old, Officer Diaz looked considerably older than the police of their earlier encounter. He wore a thick black mustache which was speckled with gray, as was his hair that was visible beneath his maroon colored beret. A black nine-millimeter pistol protruded from the tooled leather holster at his side and an M16 rifle was mounted conspicuously near the center console of his truck's cab.

Carmen sensed that **this** interrogation might not go so well.

The responses given by Carmen and the family to the officer's questions were the same as those of the previous encounter. Samuel again claimed that his family was Nicaraguan and that his preference for the English language came from his unique family background. As Abigail was being questioned, Samuel spoke with Saul attempting to reassure the anxious little boy. Without thinking Samuel slipped into speaking Portuguese, and Saul responded in kind. Abigail squeezed her husband's hand, attempting to alert him to his error, but it was too late—one of the officers had overheard the Portuguese dialogue exchange.

"Why do you speak Portuguese—you and your son also?" Officer Diaz bellowed at Samuel. "You are lying to me—you are **not** from Nicaragua."

With that, the officer ordered his team to search their packs. This time Carmen's attempt to disclaim any association with the family was in vain. Even though she possessed Nicaraguan identification, her pack was searched along with the others, and the African passports that she had been carrying for Samuel and Abigail were quickly discovered.

After inspecting the passports, Diaz looked directly at Carmen, "So, you are nothing but a filthy *coyote* (smuggler), and these *illegals* are citizens of Angola and Nigeria."

Carmen had no answer. She knew with certainty that she would be doing jail time unless she could find someone who would accept a bribe—it wouldn't be Officer Diaz.

Abigail, now sobbing uncontrollably, pleaded, "Please—please do not deport us—**please** Officer Diaz. My husband and I have traveled so far to escape from war and violence. We just want to pass through your country to reach a safe place. We just want to have a life! Please do not deport us!"

As Abigail began to describe the horrific circumstances that had prompted their flight, Officer Diaz, still smoking his cigar, listened, but he otherwise showed no reaction to her story.

When she had finished, Diaz asked quietly, "Why did you lie to me? You should have been truthful — I hate liars!"

Abigail, still sobbing replied, "I was so afraid — afraid that you would deport us. We can't go back—we can't. I am so sorry that I lied to you."

Officer Diaz, finally grinding out his cigar, stood and placed his hand gently on the sobbing woman's shoulder.

"We will take you back to our station and run a check of your identities, then we will determine what should be done with you."

Turning to Carmen he growled, "But you, *coyote*, will be spending some time in our jail.

Officer Diaz placed the pregnant mother and son in the truck's rear seat and placed Carmen and Samuel in the bed behind for the bumpy 45-minute trip.

Police headquarters was located in *Sapoa*, about 16 km away on the western edge of huge Lake Nicaragua. The city of 13,000 residents was located close enough to serve the majority of small outlying border villages and was still only 120 km from the capitol city of Managua. With its close proximity to the border, the police force in *Sapoa* processed more than their share of drug and human smugglers. The small station had six holding cells but was not equipped for the prolonged detention of migrants.

At the station, Officer Diaz directed the three family members to sit on the floor while he removed Carmen's handcuffs and locked her in one of the vacant cells.

For the next 30 minutes they sat there anxiously waiting to hear what would happen next.

The station door opened and Daniela Peña, the female officer who had apprehended them earlier, appeared carrying a plastic jug of water and a bag full of sandwiches which she offered to the grateful family.

After taking a sandwich and glass of water to Carmen in her cell, she turned to address Samuel, "Your family will sleep here on the floor tonight. Tomorrow I will escort you by bus to our detention center in Managua. You will be housed there until the authorities have conducted a check of your citizenship and criminal history. If you are found to be free of violations, you will be released and will be issued papers authorizing legal travel through our country."

"Thank you, Ms. Peña. You are so kind to bring us the food and water," Abigail said.

"Your thanks should go to my superior, Officer Diaz," she answered. "He bought the sandwiches for you!"

The grizzled senior officer must not be nearly as hard as he looked, Abi mused.

Officer Peña returned a few minutes later with several blankets. "I'm sorry, we do not have pillows for you, but these blankets should make the night a little more comfortable."

"May God bless you, Miss," Abigail replied.

Chapter 11

Centro de Albergue de Migrantes

Early the following day Officer Peña collected the family giving them time for an emotional good bye with Carmen before escorting them onto a brightly colored mini-bus. Even though the distance from *Sapoa* to *Managua* was only 120 km (74 miles), the trip would take about two hours due to frequent stops along the route and the busy traffic in central *Managua*.

Abigail and Samuel were understandably fearful about the prospect of detention, but they were hopeful that they would be processed and released quickly. God had at least spared them from deportation!

The bus had been converted, retired from service as an American school bus, and did not have the amenities of newer, more sophisticated transit buses. Whatever the condition of their transport, *it was good to be riding rather than walking*, Samuel thought, thankful that they were still heading north!

During the trip, Officer Peña continued to treat the family with kindness and respect doing her best to reassure Abigail that all would go well during their incarceration at the detention facility.

How blessed they were to be assigned to her care, thought Abigail.

Just as Officer Peña had estimated, two hours—and countless stops later, they arrived outside the gates of *Centro de Albergue de* Migrantes, the larger of two immigration detention facilities in Nicaragua. The rundown appearance of the facility attested to the fact that Nicaragua was the poorest country in Central America and the second poorest in the hemisphere.

Officer Peña escorted the family into the shabby, mint-green colored intake room and delivered transfer papers for the family to the facility's white-uniformed, intake guards. After exchanging a quick hug and a reassuring smile with Abigail, Daniela turned and walked away, returning to the waiting mini-bus.

The intake officer sat the family on a wooden bench as he reviewed their documents. After scanning their papers he explained, "Whenever possible we try to keep families with children together. Unfortunately at this time, we have no room in our family shelter. The father will be housed in one of our men's cells—the boy and his mother in the women's cell."

"Please do not separate us from my husband," Abigail pleaded!

"I'm sorry, it will have to be this way until we have a vacancy in the family unit. Your family will be put on our waiting list for the next opening."

"How long will we be kept here?" Samuel asked.

"Don't know, the officer shrugged, sometimes things move quickly—sometimes not. We are **very** crowded at this time—so many Cubans coming through here now. We currently have over 100 people living in this place!"

Samuel was taken to one of the men's "dormitories", a large open room, perhaps 1,000 sq. ft., having no furniture other than 15 or so bunkbeds. There were clearly more men here than beds so there were several men sprawled in their "claimed" spaces on the floor.

The detention officer gave Samuel a thin rolled foam mattress, advised him to find a place on the floor and offered him a small bowl of *gallo pinto* (a common bean and rice dish of Nicaragua and Costa Rica) and a bottle of water.[29]

Little notice was taken of Samuel's arrival—just another inmate being added to the overcrowded room. He found an open space near a wall not far from the entrance and rolled out his mattress. He sat there on the floor, silently eating his beans and rice while attempting to take in his new surroundings.

The room's grimy walls were covered top to bottom with messages which had been scrawled by some of the facility's prior detainees and, presumably, had been written to offer hope or express sentiment to the men that would later find themselves in this place.

From his mat on the floor, Samuel could read, *"Do not give up hope my brothers and sisters—you will get there!"* Arja from Nigeria, *"God has not forgotten us,"* Ethiopia, and *"Welcome to Hell,"* no signature. Still other messages had been penned by migrants from Iran, Cuba, Ghana, India, Pakistan, and Lebanon. These scribbles provided an amazing testament to the shared hopes of people from all across the globe to someway—somehow reach America.

From the many conversations that Samuel could hear, he knew that the ethnic mix of the facility's population must be hugely diverse. He could make out conversations being spoken in Spanish, English, Amharic, Igbo, Yoruba from Africa, and several Asian languages as well.

Having finished his meal, Samuel began chatting with some of his roommates. Many of the Spanish speakers were Cuban and, because of their unusually rapid speech, Samuel had to work hard to understand them. Even though locked up, the Cubans seemed to maintain a particularly happy demeanor. With their constant joking, they seemed to be the most fun-loving group of the lot.

Each detainee had a unique story to tell of his experience in detention and none seemed to have any idea of when they might be released. Samuel was learning that there appeared to be no consistent process, or rules that could be trusted, in predicting a detainee's term of confinement. **Much** seemed to depend on the quality of relationship that the individual's particular home country had with the government of Nicaragua. There were reports of people being processed through in as little as three days and up to more than four months. Detainees from France, Germany, Russia, Switzerland, and the USA, all who had embassies here, had normally been processed very quickly. A total of 45 countries maintained consulates in Managua which could help expedite the fates of their citizens; however, neither Angola nor Nigeria were among those countries—Samuel could not expect any help from outside these walls.

This facility was not a jail but as a detention center, strict rules and procedures were still maintained. Staff employees were courteous for the most part but not particularly friendly.

The men were allowed out of the cramped room during the day and had access to an open courtyard which was surrounded by a tall chain-link fence. A portion of the courtyard had a canvass covering that provided shelter from the sun and frequent rain.

Abigail and little Saul were placed in the women's dormitory. It was a much smaller space than the men's facility and currently housed 17 women and children, including the two new additions. Unlike the men's space, there were sufficient bunks for everyone. The women had free use of the interior but were not allowed out of the enclosed wing of the building. Abigail was told that the restriction was in place for their own protection.

She and Saul, like Samuel, had been given food, water, and bedding, but she was particularly excited to receive soap and other personal hygiene items which had been provided by benevolent Managuan churches. Neither mother nor son had bathed in days, and they were eager to use the shower. Abi's body was filthy from the grueling trek and her legs were caked with dried blood from lacerations that had been inflicted two days before.

After thoroughly scrubbing her son, Abi stood for several minutes with eyes closed, allowing the water to flood over her head and face, rejoicing as the wonderful warm water began to wash away the physical and emotional dirt of the past several days. She was confident that whatever peril might lie ahead in their journey that her God would be with them.

Two days had passed since the family first arrived at the center and Samuel had heard no news about their case. During that time, he had observed some interactions that seemed to signal progress in one's case.

About every two hours a detention officer would call out a detainee's name, then would briefly consult with that individual about some detail of their case. That consultation seemed to indicate that their particular case was, at least, being processed—a very hopeful sign.

Also once or twice a day, a name would be called and that person was ordered to gather their belongings—to be released! That was the **one** order that every detainee in the center waited anxiously to hear.

Samuel was becoming concerned. The family had now been detained four days and he still had not been called to consult with an official. Some detainees speculated that such absence of "official" interaction might signal an extended period of detention. Samuel could only hope and pray that would not be the case for his family.

It was four p.m., just an hour before their evening meal, when the cell door opened. The officer called out, "Samuel, Mr. Samuel Okotie-Eboh, gather your belongings and follow me!"

A suddenly jubilant Samuel quickly gathered his belongings and followed the officer down the long hall to the center's inmate release area. There he found Abigail and Saul anxiously waiting to greet him. The small boy jumped into his father's arms, and Abigail, with tears running down her face, threw her arms around them both weeping with joy that they had been reunited.

As the officials completed the paperwork for their release, Samuel was given three important documents—three temporary visas which would grant the family legal authorization to travel through the country.

It was a blessed day!

It was nearly six p.m. when the family finally walked out the doors of the *Centro de Albergue de* Migrantes—too late in the day to find transportation north to the Honduras border, so Samuel found directions to the city bus terminal where they could wait overnight for the next scheduled bus to the border.

Even though it was almost dark, the family decided to walk the 3.5 km to the station. Samuel had been told that they would be safe as long as they stayed on well-traveled streets.

The directions that he had been given seemed quite odd. "Walk to the left until you come to a round-a-bout with a statue of a man on a horse. Turn left and follow the big street called *Pista Larreynega*, walking against the one-way traffic. There will probably be no street sign," and so on. Managua navigation was, for the most part, void of street names or proper address numbers. Locations were referenced to all sorts of landmarks—trees, colorful buildings—sometimes even abandoned cars were cited for navigation purposes.

It had apparently been that way ever since a powerful earthquake had destroyed the city back in 1972. It had just never recovered in any structured way. For a large city (2.2 million residents), it was strange that very few buildings were higher than one-story tall. The low skyline made it even more difficult for the family to pick out visible features to help establish direction.

The family hadn't eaten at all since the morning meal and were now quite hungry. A street vendor close by was selling a dish that looked delicious and had a wonderful aroma but was unfamiliar to the African couple. Samuel handed the vendor C$45 ($1.50 USD), for two piping hot plates of *Quesillo* (a classic Nicaraguan dish) that was especially popular in Managua, consisting of cheese, onions, cream, vinegar and potatoes wrapped in a corn tortilla and grilled over open flame.

The family found a convenient wooden bench nearby where they could rest and enjoy their steaming Quesillo before continuing on their walk to the terminal.

Moving on, they reached the final landmark described in their directions. Another traffic circle—this one, unmistakable.

The *Hugo Chávez Eternal Commander Rotonda* was dominated by three of *La Avenida Bolivar's* 22 massive metal, metallic gold trees and sat in front of a giant multicolored steel caricature of the former Venezuelan President. The entire scene was illuminated by hundreds of small lights that were sprinkled throughout the trees. Such a memorial, built to honor a *Venezuelan* in Nicaragua, seemed strange but apparently Chavez was considered a hero of Latin America.[30]

It had taken the family about an hour to reach Managua's *Mercado Mayoreo* bus station. Like most buildings in Managua, the station was single level and was constructed of square steel columns which supported an expansive corrugated metal roof. The building had no side walls, so the interior space was completely open and exposed to weather and bus fumes. The gray concrete floor slab did offer several rows of benches which very closely resembled bench seats found in older model domestic vans.

Samuel found a ticket office still open and was able to purchase tickets scheduled for the morning's first bus to the Guesaule border crossing to Honduras. The station's narrow benches would not offer the family much comfort for sleeping, but at least the family should be safe for the night.

Abigail pulled her knees up against her pregnant belly and slumped back against the seat. Using his pack for a pillow, Samuel lay alongside her on the concrete floor with Saul, already asleep, on the bench above him.

Morning came early at the station. With buses scheduled to leave as early as 7 a.m., the daily bustle had begun around an hour earlier. Departing buses were being staged at the foot of the elevated concrete pad, and throngs of travelers were arriving to board the aging vehicles for destinations all across the country.

Unlike the individual terminals run by the more expensive premier bus lines such as *Tica*, buses that served this terminal, *ruteados,* were commonly known as "chicken-buses." The term, used to describe buses which had been converted from retired American school bus service to inter-city use, came from the fact that farm animals (chickens) were often transported along with the human passengers. Virtually all *ruteados* were painted in bright colors, with no two designs or color schemes the same.

Samuel purchased fried sweet plantains, some white bread, and water from one of the station's numerous vendors to take along for breakfast. Their bus, scheduled to depart at 7:45, was already in the process of loading.

The trip to *Guesaule* would require transferring buses at two locations along the route—one at Leon and the second at Chinandega. If everything went as scheduled, they would arrive at the border by noon.

The *Guesaule* bound bus was painted in lively colors as were all of the chicken-buses around the terminal. Not a square inch of surface was without the brightly colored paint. The front cab area was painted with a mural depicting a cathedral which was staged against a backdrop of snow-covered mountains. Even the top half of the driver's windshield was painted over, apparently to block the glare of low sun, and the sides of the bus were covered with graphics that seemed to have no relationship at all to adjacent themes.

Samuel followed Abi and Saul as they climbed up onto the bus and turned down the aisle past the "alter-like" driver's area. It was quite common for bus drivers in South America to decorate their cab with all manner of religious objects, statues, rosaries, etc. to enlist God's protection while traveling— this driver was no exception.

Having been among the first passengers to board, the family found seats together near the back. After stowing their packs and breakfast in the overhead rack, the three settled in for the trip north.

The bus's seats were occupied, so passengers that boarded late, or were less aggressive, were left to ride standing in the crowded aisle.

At 8:15 the bus, packed to overflowing with its daily cargo of sweaty humanity and rooftop rack loaded with baggage, sacks of rice, and crates of live chickens, pulled away from the platform and began the two hour trip down the Pan American Highway to Leon.

Chapter 12

Honduras to Guatemala

Abigail sat near the open window. Nearly all of the sliding windows were open since there was no air conditioning, and the unpleasant odors of sweaty bodies encouraged as much ventilation as possible. Samuel sat on the outside in order to spare his wife from the unavoidable body contact with standing passengers who were jostled back and forth in the narrow aisle.

Although there were no designated bus stops other than the destination city, Leon, the driver made frequent stops, to allow passengers to leave or others to board, at any location along the route. *Ruteado* drivers never passed up a fare and there was no such thing as too many passengers—so it was not uncommon to see busses with people hanging from the sides, rooftop, or rear bumper. *Ruteado* fares were quite inexpensive and were determined by the specific travel distance of each customer.

An hour into the trip, Samuel retrieved their bread and plantains from the rack above, and the family ate their breakfast. Samuel needn't have been concerned about food on the trip because at every stop near a major town, hordes of vendors would push their way onto the bus, selling everything from fried chicken to nail clippers—just to get off at the next stop and board another bus to do it again.

After changing busses at Leon, the family continued on toward their last bus change in Chinandega. Unlike the first bus which had blared loud *"ranchera"* style music for the entire trip, this bus featured a traveling preacher who stood at the front preaching about Jesus to anyone who would listen.[31]

Abigail was amazed at how cordial the passengers remained. Even though the crowded bus was hot, loud, and uncomfortable — she never heard one person complain.

Samuel ushered his family off the bus when they reached *Somotillo* (a town of 30,000 people) 4 km before the *Guesaule* border crossing, knowing that the family's next challenge would be crossing the border into Honduras. He was not certain yet just how that would be accomplished, but they would spend the night here and address that problem tomorrow.

Samuel found an inexpensive hotel, the *El Paso Real*, just a few blocks from the bus stop and checked the family in. It was likely to be the last night, for some time, that the three would enjoy a decent bed and comfortable shelter. Whatever unknown circumstances were yet to unfold for them on this journey, they were bound to be challenging.

That evening Samuel sat chatting with two local men whom he had met in a small coffee shop nearby. Eventually working up the courage to divulge to them, his intention to cross the border, he found that the sensitive topic came as no surprise. *Somotillo's* close proximity to the border had brought many such immigrants through the town.

Samuel was heartened to learn that the travel visas they had been given by Nicaraguan authorities would likely be honored by Honduran immigration authorities as well. It appeared that the country's current policy was to continue pushing the flow of illegal migration north rather than have countless displaced people stacking up within their own borders.

Samuel's confidants from the coffee shop recommended that the family turn themselves in to authorities at the border, present their African passports along with their Nicaraguan travel visas, and request passage through Honduras with the intent to reach Canada. According to the men, immigration had been issuing such migrants one-week travel permits and allowing them to cross the border.

This was wonderful news! At least for tomorrow, the outlook for a successful border crossing looked promising.

The **real** challenge, the men said, would come later—at the Guatemalan border.

At 10 p.m. the following day, just as their new friends had recommended, Samuel and Abi got into the entry line at *Guesaule's* border crossing planning to present their African passports and Nicaraguan travel visas to the Honduran border authorities. The couple trusted that the locals had given them reliable information but remained keenly aware that they were still at risk for deportation.

Even though there were not too many people ahead of them, it was taking forever for the pedestrian entry line to inch forward. The couple attempted to remain calm and positive while contending with their impatient three-year-old

Finally, they reached the immigration counter; holding their breath as the officer reviewed their documents. He did not ask the couple any questions at all, which Samuel thought peculiar. After scrutinizing their papers, the officer began to make entries on an official-looking form that he had pulled from beneath the counter. Samuel feared that this form might well be a deportation order.

When the officer had completed the form, he tore off the bottom copy and handed it to Samuel, mechanically stating, "Your family has seven days to legally move through our country. If you are apprehended here after that time you will be arrested and immediately deported." With that, and never looking up, he unceremoniously waved the family across the border into Honduras.

From the border check point, the three were able to hitch a ride in the bed of a large truck to the city of *Guesaule*. From there they caught a *ruteado* which was headed northwest to the capitol city of *Tecucigalpa*. There they would transfer busses and then travel on to the city of *Sante Fe*, just a few miles south of the Guatemalan border. The entire trip across Honduras, about 560 km, would take, at best, the remainder of the day.

The couple was grateful to God that they had made it through immigration into Honduras successfully but knew full well that crossing the border into Guatemala would be their greatest test yet.

Abigail was now almost eight months pregnant. The physically taxing, anxiety filled days were becoming more difficult for her—Toronto still seemed so very far away. The couple had heard many horrible stories of migrants that had attempted to make the brutal mountain trek between Honduras and Guatemala and feared that it might become the only option for them as well.

It was well past dark, around nine p.m. when the bus made its stop in *Sante Fe*. The tired family made their way off the bus and shuffled down the street toward an open-air market hoping to inquire about shelter for the night.

Early the next morning, after spending the night in the annex of a Catholic church where the priest graciously allowed them to sleep, Samuel left his family and set out to find a man named Gustavo. He had been told that this man, a produce vendor at the town market, was rumored to help people who were *without documents* cross the border into Guatemala. Samuel could only hope that this Gustavo would prove to be as trustworthy and helpful as he had been told.

Many vendors sold produce at the bustling city market, but only one vendor clearly matched the description that Samuel had been given.

Samuel approached the open air stall, noting that it was not all that different from the auto parts stall that he and his father had operated back in Nigeria.

"Buenos días, ¿estás Gustavo," he asked.

The middle-aged man had a kind but weathered face. The deep creases in his face and darkly tanned skin attested to many years of working outdoors.

"Sí, me llamo Gustavo, por qué pedís (yes, my name is Gustavo, why do you ask)?" the man replied.

"My name is Samuel. My family is traveling north to Canada and we are looking for someone that can help us to cross the border. I was told that you might be able to assist us."

"Perhaps," said Gustavo, carefully considering Samuel. "It is not an easy thing and very dangerous. There are thieves that must be avoided and the route over the mountains is hard. It cannot be done without the use of horses."

"Horses? We have never even been close to a horse!" Samuel exclaimed. "It is just me, my wife, and our three-year-old son—and my wife is **very** pregnant. I don't know if she could even get up onto a horse."

"It may be too difficult then, but there is no other way. I am sorry my friend!"

Samuel, crestfallen to learn of this unexpected circumstance, turned to walk back to the church and deliver the disappointing news to Abigail.

As he had expected, Abigail was disappointed, but she was determined to attempt the crossing, no matter the difficulty.

"Samuel, we have come too far to turn back now. I can do it—Saul can do it. Even if we need a horse, I can do the ride over the mountains. I will do whatever I need to do!"

"It will be too hard on you and the baby. The trail will be very rough and you would both be risking injury," argued Samuel. "We could even lose the baby!"

"Samuel, we have to go **now!** We can't stay here any longer. I'm not going to have our baby in Guatemala. We can at least get to America before the baby comes."

Samuel had seen this *determined* look on Abigail's face before. There was no argument that would change her mind. The family **would** be attempting the dangerous crossing. With Abigail's risks increasing daily, there was no time to waste; they would be leaving tonight.

Gustavo accepted the job, duly noting that he had warned the couple in regard to the hazards involved, and he would not be held responsible for the physical safety of the pregnant mother and baby.

Just before dark, Gustavo parked his old pickup truck in the dirt lot outside of the church. Samuel tossed their bags into the truck bed while Abi scooted across the narrow bench seat sitting in the middle next to Gustavo. Samuel squeezed into the cramped cab next to his wife, lifted Saul onto his lap, and the truck headed west out of *Sante Fe* toward the border.

They would depart, on this adventure, from a ranch located about eight km west of the *Corinto* border crossing—the most westerly located of Guatemala's three immigration stations. The ranch was owned by Gustavo's "business partner" as were the three horses they would be riding. For this his partner would be receiving a generous share of the smuggling fee—as usual.

The remote property's barbed wire fence backed right up against the mountain's tree line and actually paralleled the country's shared border with Guatemala. Gustavo's plan for tonight's journey would be uncomplicated as usual. He would leave the pickup at the ranch, lead his clients over the mountain into Guatemala on horseback and return to reclaim the truck sometime the following day.

Gustavo's partner had fed and watered the horses, but it was Gustavo's job to get them saddled. He accomplished this using the only light source available, the truck headlights. After saddling the horses, he secured the family's packs to the rear of the saddles, and then turned his attention to getting the reluctant riders on board.

Abi and Samuel were already nervous being so close to the massive unfamiliar animals, and Saul was sharing their anxiety—but the family was committed; they would soon confront their fears and climb up onto these towering, snorting animals.

Gustavo thought it best to put Abigail on Bella, a seal-brown, 20-year-old mare. Bella was the oldest of the three horses but also the calmest. Gustavo held the reins while Samuel boosted Abigail up onto Bella's worn leather saddle. He then adjusted Bella's stirrups and placed the reins into Abigail's shaking hands.

"Don't worry Abigail," Gustavo assured her, "your only job is to hold on and hold her reins. Bella knows what to do—she is trained to follow my horse and do whatever my horse does; stop, go, turn. You will be fine!"

Aided by the now dimming light of the truck's headlights, Samuel lifted his frightened son onto the bay-colored horse which was tethered behind Abigail's. His horse, also a mare, was a beautiful reddish-brown color with a black mane, tail, and lower legs.

Gingerly, Samuel put his foot into the stirrup and pulled himself up onto the saddle behind his son. Wrapping one arm around Saul and grasping the reins with the other he said, "It's ok son, Daddy's got you"—and, trying to convince himself as well as his boy, he added, "It will be **fun** to ride the nice horsey."

With his clients successfully mounted behind him, Gustavo shut off the truck lights, locked the door, and climbed onto the lead horse, Macho. The stout gray gelding was not a particularly beautiful animal, but in spite of missing some private parts, he carried himself with the air of being the top horse in this string.

With the simple instruction, "OK, we go!" Gustavo gently clamped his knees into the gelding's flanks and commanded "*paso*" (walk). The string of horses sauntered across the moonlit field and disappeared into the tree line that marked the beginning of their journey.

Chapter 13

Grueling Passage

By skirting to the west and well outside of the highly patrolled *Corinto* border crossing, Gustavo hoped to avoid any encounter with the police. This route would take them into the thick protected forests of the *Trifinio Biosphere Reserve,* a mountainous expanse of 221 km² (85 sq. mi.). *Montecristo*, at almost 8,000 ft. elevation, was its tallest peak. The mountain's cloud forest was made up of massive oak and laurel trees up to 30 meters tall, and was home to rare wildlife species like pumas, anteaters and spider monkeys. Unfortunately, its remote trails were also utilized by vicious drug cartels and illegal tree harvesters who, like Gustavo himself, exploited the minimal police presence of the region.

The Mexican drug cartel, the Zetas, were known to transport cocaine through this area as well as trafficking throughout all of Guatemala, Colombia, and Mexico.

A particularly worrisome group was *Mara Salvatrucha* (MS-13), an international criminal gang that originated in Los Angeles, California but had now spread to other parts of the United States, Canada, Mexico, and Central America. The, originally Salvadoran, gang was now composed of an ethnic mix of Central Americans but were especially active in Guatemala. Members of MS could be identified by tattoos covering their entire body (and often the face), as well as the use of their own sign language. The "*Maras*" notorious reputation for use of violence and cruel revenge earned them recruitment, as partners, by the Sinaloa Cartel who were battling against Los Zetas for control of the area.[32]

The possibility of encountering these criminals was minimal, but any possibility at all was a legitimate concern. Gustavo crossed himself, praying that he and the young family would not be running into any of those characters tonight. He had experienced some very close calls in the past, but he had not yet been robbed by thieves or apprehended by the police.

As the riders began their trek into the reserve, they would be climbing from an elevation of 819 m (2,687 ft.) at the tree line to about 6,000 ft. at the trail's summit, before dropping down the other side. Assuming that they were successful in making the trek, the party would break out of the forest before first light, well inside the

Guatemalan border, and somewhere near the city of *Esquipulas*.

Gustavo's horse, *Macho*, led the trio up the rocky trail with the family's two horses in line behind. The three horses required no guidance at this point, because the trail was narrow, with thick trees and rocks on both sides, leaving no option as to direction of travel. Attempting to move too quickly in the darkness and difficult terrain would make anything faster than a walk, perilous for both horse and rider, so their pace would remain slow and constant. The three horses had made this trip many times before, so they were familiar with the terrain. Their keen senses and superior eyesight in darkness gave them a significant advantage over their human riders.

Gustavo rarely spoke as the party wound their way up the treacherous, serpentine trail. So for the past two hours, the only sounds made had been the breathing of the horses and the clatter of hooves on rocky ground.

Saul whimpered in discomfort as he bounced between the saddle horn and against his father's thighs behind, his little legs spread wide in order to span the adult-sized saddle. Samuel's arm was cramping from the continual effort required to keep his son from bouncing off the horse. Abigail had been stoic as usual, but Samuel knew that she must be hurting from every jarring step up the mountain.

As their horses threaded their way through the thick underbrush, low hanging branches hidden in the darkness slapped at the rider's faces, while endless patches of thorny overgrown brush tore at their legs.

The constantly twisting trail was treacherous in spots, with $180°$ turns and steep rocky steps.

Gustavo had instructed the riders to lean forward with stirrups back, as much as possible, in order to shift their body weight and help the horses climb.

Abi's pregnant belly made riding in this position extremely uncomfortable. She was already experiencing sharp pains in her abdomen and back from the unnatural posture and relentless pounding.

Alert to his wife's discomfort, Samuel advised Gustavo that they must stop and rest. Gustavo halted *Macho*, and the other horses followed suit. Samuel swung his leg over to dismount, shocked by how stiff and sore that he had become so early into the ride. He lifted his boy to the ground then moved up to Abi's horse to help her down.

Abi took a deep breath and sat there quietly for a moment. Then with eyes closed, she said, "Samuel I need a minute. I will need to do this *very* slowly, please."

She gingerly stood up in the stirrups, cautiously trying to lift her leg over the saddle, then cried out, "ooooah—Samuel, there is so much pain!"

Samuel grabbed her gently below her buttocks and took as much of her weight as she could tolerate until she could slide her opposite leg over the saddle and step down.

He held her there in the darkness as she trembled, sobbing quietly and overcome with worry about the health of her unborn child.

Realizing how greatly distressed that Abi had become, Samuel's mind raced as he frantically considered their options. They had ridden less than a third of the distance to their destination and Abigail was already suffering terribly.

"Abi, we can't go on. It is too hard on you — you and the baby!"

"I will be alright," Abi declared — "if I can just rest for a few minutes. We **can't** go back. We have to go on — we **must** go on!"

This was exactly the situation that Gustavo had feared, getting part way through the journey and having this pregnant woman unable to proceed.

He removed a thick wool Guatemalan blanket that had been secured behind his saddle and folded it to create a makeshift saddle cushion. He then lashed the blanket to Abi's saddle using nylon cordage from his saddle bags.

The party rested there in the dark for another 20 minutes before hoisting themselves back onto their mounts. It had required all of Abi's strength to remount her horse, but she found Gustavo's improvised cushion provided some welcome relief from the hard saddle.

They continued up the mountain, almost always rising in altitude. Occasionally, the trail would level off or even descend for a short distance, but in these spots they found running streams, with slick rocks to cross, that required extra caution even with the sure footed horses.

The highland areas of Guatemala, between 3,000 and 6,000 ft. of elevation, were the more temperate zones of the country. Even at this date in late December, it was considered summer with daytime temperatures around 85°F (30°C) and nights most often quite cool. As the group climbed in elevation and the hour became later, the temperatures correspondingly dropped.

The cooler temperatures were good for the horses, but it was starting to be uncomfortably cool for the lightly dressed riders. Fortunately, back in *Sante Fe,* Abigail had found some stretch pants that she could wear, so her legs were somewhat warmer and better protected than during their earlier night-time trek over the Costa Rica-Nicaraguan border.

Summer months here were typically dryer than winters, which could be very wet, but the country had been known to experience torrential rains in any month of the year.

Gustavo was becoming somewhat concerned as he spotted intermittent lightning flashes off in the distant west. The area's most severe storms came in from the west after sweeping in off of the Pacific Ocean.

The thought of being stuck in a storm half way up the mountain on a dark rocky trail, with responsibility for a frightened little boy, a pregnant mother and her frantic husband—all of them inexperienced riders, would not be a good thing!

The only option was to press on in hopes that the storm would stall or change direction. Nothing could be gained by stopping now.

The group had been climbing for over four hours and were now at almost 6,000 ft. of elevation. In another half-hour they would crest the summit and begin the less exhausting descent.

Gustavo had been counting the number of seconds between flashes and the rumble of thunder that followed. The interval was down to 3 seconds, so he calculated the approaching storm to be no farther than one-half mile away. There was not enough time for them to reach the summit before the storm hit, so the best they could do was to dismount, secure the horses, and attempt to put up a small shelter.

Gustavo lifted the little boy down from Samuel's horse, then helped Samuel gently lower Abi to the ground. She was in bad shape, having suffered some bleeding from the trauma of the pounding ride.

Samuel was desperate with concern to protect his wife and son— this was his job, his responsibility to keep them safe—but in this situation, it seemed that there was nothing he could do.

Abi pulled Saul into her arms, cradling him in her lap on the ground, while Samuel helped Gustavo put up a small tarp that he carried for such emergencies. The two men quickly tied the tarp's corners to low hanging tree branches, hoping that the covering would offer at least some protection from the downpour that was about to come.

It was no more than a minute before the edge of the storm arrived. The rain started slowly at first but quickly become a deluge. Water poured onto the tarp from the trees above and streamed off the lower side, becoming a river below their feet. Samuel huddled on the ground next to Abi and his son, with Gustavo squeezed in closely beside him—this small covering had never been intended to shelter four people.

Although they were partially protected from the barrage of water from above, they could do nothing to stop the water that poured across the ground beneath them. In minutes the ground had become muddy, and their pants were soaked through from the bottom.

After 20 minutes the intensity of the rain had not diminished. Gustavo knew that storms such as this could last for hours. During the momentary flashes of lightning, he could see that the torrential flow of water was rapidly flooding the trail. The route here passed through a ravine that had been cut through the rocky mountainside by just such powerful torrents of rushing water. Gustavo feared that if the storm continued they could be trapped here in the path of a flash flood.

It was rapidly becoming too dangerous to stay here. The trail could become completely impassable, and they were not prepared to be stuck at this high elevation for a prolonged period. Like it or not, they had no choice—they would have to continue on and hope that the storm would pass behind them.

Gustavo had one more useful item in his saddle bags. He dashed out to his horse and returned with several plastic garbage bags. He gave three to the family members and showed them how to modify the bags for use as rain ponchos.

Samuel was sick with worry. He knew that they must move on or risk being swept away if the ravine should suddenly flood, but Abigail's condition was becoming desperate. Her bleeding was the most alarming concern. *Had she lost the baby or caused injury to the baby or herself?* Neither parent was expert in the complications of pregnancy but both were fearful that the ride's relentless jarring could have caused harm to the fragile placenta.

With his face streaming wet with tears and rain, Samuel cried out to the lightning filled sky, "God, please God, take me. I would rather die here now on this mountain than have anything happen to my wife or babies. I cannot bear to see my wife suffer. God, please protect my wife and babies!"

Abigail pulled Samuel into her embrace and held him tightly, and with her face pressed against his she whispered, *"The people that walked in darkness have seen a great light; those that dwell in the land of the shadow of death, upon them has the light shined."* Isaiah 9:2

"Samuel, the lightning is telling us that God is still with us; shining on us—even in this shadow of death he is with us. He is our light, and he will protect us."

The four riders put on the make-shift ponchos, took down the tarp, and once again, in the driving rain, climbed back onto their wet horses.

Soon the party had ridden out of the long ravine and away from the threat of flash flood danger. The terrain's slick rocks now alternated with deep muddy furrows that had been carved by the flow of rushing water. The horses struggled with footing, becoming tentative with each step and unsure of the treacherous surface.

Finally, more than an hour behind schedule, the riders reached the crest of the trail and began the descent. The downhill going was somewhat easier on Abigail. She could now lean back to help her horse with weight distribution and reduce the impact on her abdomen as well; even so, she winced with pain at every step.

The horses often faltered as they grappled with the steep, slick terrain. Each misstep of Abi's horse, followed by the jolting recovery, sent waves of pain through her body.

She tried not to think about the pain, staying focused on remembering that every step down the trail brought them closer to relief, rest, and safety. *She could make it — she could make it,* she told herself.

The storm had passed, and the trail was becoming less treacherous, allowing their pace to pick up a bit as the ground became less steep. In an hour, they would reach *Río Atulapa,* a river that flowed to the east out of the mountains. They planned to follow the river out of the thick forest and on to the city of *Esquipulas*, which was located well inside the Guatemalan border.

As they approached the river, the trail began to flatten out and the overgrowth became less dense. The level ground was a welcome relief to both horse and rider, but the thinning vegetation would leave them more exposed and any noise they made would carry a great distance without the muffling of thick forest growth.

Visibility was now also a concern. As an unfortunate result of the storm delays, it was becoming light. Gustavo was nervous that they would be completing the trip in daylight.

Making more noise than they would like, the riders followed the river downstream. The clatter of horse hooves on the riverbank's smooth stones was unavoidable. *The river was beautiful,* Abigail thought; *a place that she would love to spend more time if the circumstances were different.* The fast moving water was remarkably clear, and she found the sounds that it made as it rushed around the large boulders protruding from its surface to be soothing and therapeutic. This was the first moment since they had left the ranch the previous evening that she had felt a degree of calmness—but what was that sound, now barely detectable above the noise of the rustling river?

They had almost reached the point where Gustavo would be leaving them to continue on foot to *Esquipulas* when the Toyota police vehicle appeared out of the trees 100 meters away. The black pick-up, with its bright yellow stripe and large DSCP-058 identification on the side, was unmistakably a National Civilian Police truck. Two officers rode inside, and a third officer was standing in the bed, holding tightly to the grab-bar with one hand and gesturing wildly to them with the other.

Chapter 14

Rio Suchiate to Mexico

Gustavo was the first to recognize the distinctive black and yellow truck. Its roof carried the distinctive red, white, and blue light bar which was now quite visible. He had feared this possibility, especially with the party being totally exposed by full daylight. *It could have been worse though*, he thought, *these men could have been members of Mara Salvatrucha or one of the other brutal drug gangs.*

Abigail's heart sank. They had come so close to the end of this grueling journey and now they were about to be apprehended by the police—again. Again? How many times would God have them go through this experience? They would surely be deported this time.

The Guatemalan PNC officers wore fitted military-style black uniforms and black berets with a gold shield on the side—*appearing much more intimidating than the Nicaraguan police*, thought Abigail.

The officer in charge reviewed their documents and confirmed their illegal status in short order—this time the couple did not attempt to claim otherwise. Gustavo, who after numerous similar encounters had become familiar with the game, was the first to suggest that a monetary deal (a bribe) might be made in exchange for their release.

As Gustavo had guessed, the officer was receptive. After each of the party had paid a $200 (1500 Quetzal) bribe, Gustavo was released and, with his three borrowed horses, turned back the way he had come—back to the Honduran border.

The family learned that they must still go back to the police station in *Esquipulas*. Samuel explained to the officer that Abigail was in desperate need of medical attention, but the office just shrugged, saying that the station was not equipped to provide medical aid; they would need to look for help elsewhere.

This was becoming a case of *deja vu* for the couple. Here they were *again* in the bed of a police truck, and even though they had paid a *fine*, they were unsure of what would happen to them next.

The bumpy ride from the river bank into the town of *Esquipulas* was as punishing for Abi as the horseback ride had been, and Samuel could do nothing to ease her pain. Finally they arrived at the police station, grateful to climb out of the stiffly-sprung pickup truck bed.

The family was ushered into a station room and the door was locked behind them. The room was bare except for wooden benches that lined the walls. Slumped on the benches sat six bedraggled-looking men, who looked as tired and disoriented as they must themselves. After a short conversation with the men, Samuel learned that they were Cubans who had been arrested the previous night, also, for entering the country illegally, and none of them had heard what would happen to them next.

The family had been detained in the room for about an hour when the door opened. The police officer, not one that they had seen before, ordered all nine detainees outside and escorted them back to the rear of the building.

Abigail was worried—this officer was not among the three that had taken their money at the river.

The officer led them out to a bus that sat parked in the dusty gravel driveway, engine running, and directed them to get in.

Abigail, now terrified that they were being deported, cried out to the officer, "No! No!—we paid the man—the other police man! They said they would let us go! They promised to let us go!—and now you deport us?"

"Señora," the officer said, "the bus will take you to the immigration station at *Corinto*. There you will all be given documents that allow you to pass through our country. You will not be deported."

The nine migrants climbed onto the bus, joining several others already aboard, who were being bussed to *Corinto* for the same purpose.

Abigail collapsed into a seat with her little boy and Samuel beside her. A flood of relief, at learning that her family would *not* be deported, left her elated but utterly spent. Neither Samuel nor Abi spoke on the ride to the immigration station, each being content to process this latest experience in silence.

By the end of the day, immigration authorities had processed the family's documents and issued them travel visas as promised.

With visas in hand, the family hitchhiked to the *Esquipulas* bus station where Samuel purchased tickets to transport them across Guatemala to the Mexican border.

Fares on the *Bus Trans Galgos Inter* line were far less expensive than those of major carriers, but with stops in *Guatemala City*, *Plaza Barrios*, and *Antigua*, this option required seven hours of additional travel time. Although not as plush as busses of the premier lines, the *Inter* line bus was much more comfortable than the *ruteados* had been in Nicaragua and the terminals at each of their stops were clean.

The terminal's bathroom provided the opportunity for the family to freshen up and change their clothes for the first time in days. Samuel even gave his son Saul a sponge bath.

The 17-hour bus ride across the country was allowing time for the family to recover from their harrowing trip over the mountains, and Samuel was hopeful that Abi's beaten body could use this time to heal.

His plan was to get off the bus at the town of *Tecún Umán* on the Honduras side of the border and find a guide who could help them cross *Rio Suchiate* (the river that marks the boundary of Guatemala and Mexico at this location in the Mexican state of Chiapas).

Samuel and his family, like thousands of other migrants, were caught in an unfortunate game of *hot potato* that was being played out within the chain of countries from South America to Mexico. Each of these countries, unwilling to absorb the financial burden of detaining, housing, and feeding the staggering flow of illegal immigrants, were quickly processing them, issuing them temporary visas, and sending them on to become the problem of the next country.

Samuel knew that if they attempted to pass through the border check point with Mexico, they would be turned back, but if they could successfully get across the river and turn themselves into Mexican immigration in *Ciudad Hidalgo*, they could apply for temporary travel papers.

After stepping off the bus in *Tecún Umán,* the family began to walk the three short blocks down to the *Suchiate* River. Only the main street was paved, and as they turned downhill toward the water the narrow street became hard-packed clay. The town had grown to a population of 30,000 people with much of the growth coming from con-men and hustlers who had been drawn here seeking to *cash in* on the human trafficking or the movement of illegal contraband across the border. *Tecún Umán* had become known as "Little Tijuana," a vice-filled haven for disreputable characters of all sorts.[33]

It was a bizarre scene that greeted them as they reached the river edge, with a frenzy of activity all around. Just beneath the border-bridge above, men were unloading food products, beer, large containers of gasoline, and other domestic items from huge plank-decked truck inner tubes (*balsas*). The cargo had been rafted over from Mexico where the items were much cheaper. On the return trip the rafts would carry human cargo or drugs headed north.[34]

All of this illegal activity was happening in plain sight of Mexican authorities who were stationed just a short distance upriver at the official border crossing. The authorities took little notice of the tattered migrants who they observed jumping off of the rafts and onto the banks on the Mexican side, knowing that if they apprehended them, they would be obliged to feed and house them.

As the family approached the flotilla of rafts, they were swarmed by shirtless young men, all clamoring to transport them across the river to the Mexican side. Samuel quickly selected one raft operator, Hector—who had been less aggressive than the others—and paid him $4.50 to raft them across the wide muddy river.

This raft, like all the others, consisted of two huge truck inner tubes which had been lashed together, and was topped by thin wooden planks which served as a crude cargo deck—the only differentiation from other rafts being its name, *malu*, which was spray-painted in magenta on the tube sides.

Since the family had only their backpacks to carry, loading was a simple process. Hector instructed them to sit down near the center of the wooden deck, then he began to push the raft away from the shore and into the current of the flowing river. Once away from the bank, he pulled himself up onto the rear of the deck platform and grabbed the long wooden pole that he would use to push the raft across.

He planted the end of the pole firmly into the river bottom near the rear of the raft, then pushing hard against it, he launched the raft toward the opposite bank. By repeating this alternating sequence of poling and gliding, it took Hector about 25 minutes to pole his fares across the 200-meter-wide river.

The whole episode seemed surreal to Samuel. Here they were on a raft in the process of making an **illegal** border crossing, and doing so in broad daylight and within clear view of unconcerned authorities. It was strange, to be sure.

When they reached the river's edge on the Mexican side, Hector used the pole to wedge the raft firmly against the rocky bank.

Samuel was the first to scramble off, carrying Saul. After putting his boy safely onto the bank, he returned to help Abi step from the bobbing raft deck onto large boulders that lined the water's edge. Before the family had fully gathered themselves on the bank, Hector was already headed back across the river, hoping to find more paying customers.

The rocky shoreline transitioned into tall grass and thick brush as they climbed up the hillside and away from the river. The feet of countless migrants who had walked this route before them had worn a clear path through the undergrowth, so they followed the path until they came out of the brush and onto a dirt road that paralleled the river.

Samuel knew that if they followed the road north for a short distance, they should run right into the *Cuidad Hidalgo* Mexican Immigration station where they planned to turn themselves in. He knew that the Mexican authorities would be obligated to process them now that they had crossed into Mexico. Their objective was to obtain temporary Mexican visas, as they had been granted from previous countries, which would allow them to, legally, continue their journey north.

The family reached the Immigration station a half-hour later, and after waiting in a short line, they presented their documents to the official at the counter. The immigration agent, here in Mexico, was not a police officer or even border patrol. His job was, simply, to certify citizenship and deal with immigration issues.

The agent accepted the visas and birth certificates presented by Abigail and Samuel but was skeptical of the authenticity of their son's papers. Saul's birth certificate had never been questioned before, so this was a new problem.

"I have never seen a birth certificate like this one," he said. "And I find it hard to believe that such a little child has traveled all the way from Angola!"

"He was born in Angola, but we lived for several months in Brazil. He has made the entire journey with us, walking, riding on horseback, everything with us," Abigail countered.

"I am not convinced that the boy **is** actually your son. Many people attempt to smuggle children across the border for all kinds of bad purposes—they do it for the money."

"I am going to send you to *Estación Migratoria Siglo XXI* in *Tapachula*. We will have to hold you while we do a DNA test to determine if he is your son."

"Please Sir, the boy is our son! We are only wanting to pass through your country to have a better life for our son. My sister is waiting for us in Canada!"

"I'm sorry Señora, you will all be taken to our detention center until we can confirm your information."

Before the end of the day, the family had been put on a dust covered Immigration bus and were headed for *Tapachula*, about 30 km away.

Chapter 15

Tales of Terror

Estación *Migratoria* *Siglo* *XXI* (21st Century Immigration Station), a clean modern complex, with a capacity for 960 men, women and children, and the largest of 48 permanent detention centers in Mexico, was currently operating at full capacity due to the recent influx of immigrants. This center alone had processed 114,000 detentions this year.[35]

It was late afternoon, Friday December 11th, when the family began their intake process at the facility. Samuel noted that, unlike Nicaragua's detention center, all the employees here were unarmed—appearing more like social workers than jailers.

It soon became evident that the family would be split up again, as they had been in Nicaragua. Abigail and Saul would be sent to the woman's dormitory and Samuel to the men's. Abi was understandably upset, but she was hopeful that the question of Saul's parentage would be quickly answered.

The women's dorm attendant, a stocky young Mexican woman, wearing the center's non-descript kaki colored uniform, issued Abi a plastic bag containing personal hygiene items. After making it *very clear* that any future soap or other items would have to be purchased from the facility's store, she promptly escorted mother and son to the women's dorm. The pregnant woman still had not been physically examined or offered any medical care but was grateful to have the personal hygiene items and access to washing facilities.

The dorm's large sleeping area was packed with, perhaps, 100 women whose noisy conversations competed with the din of small children that were playing nearby. The facility did have a small game room and library which might make Saul's stay here more pleasant.

Two days later, the immigration staff *finally* took cheek swabs from the mother and son. Many women had been confined here for as much as three months with no clear expectation of their release status. Abi was hopeful that the DNA test results, which would confirm their genetic relationship, would be processed quickly so that they could be released.

As Abigail shared her story with some of the women, she learned that many of their experiences were very much like her own. She found that the sharing of these emotional stories and the trials that these women had overcome were both therapeutic and inspiring.

The women had all been moved to immigrate by a common desire—simply to seek safety and a better life—nothing fancy— just to be safe, to have freedom, to live life. By now, they knew that there was no guarantee they would even make it to the *Promised Land*. Waiting before them were a host of dangers, some worse than those already experienced.

Unscrupulous Mexican officials, rather than engaging in crude violence, typically demanded *mordidas* (bribes). The payments varied from a few dollars to allow a single person across the border, or thousands of dollars to permit drugs, weapons, stolen automobiles, or other illegal contraband to pass through. Mexican criminals often kidnaped northbound travelers, held them for ransom while demanding payment from their families, or sometimes even raped or killed them.[36] At least 11,000 migrants had disappeared the past year alone while attempting to travel north through the country. Those that had come through Guatemala, prior to reaching Mexico, had typically been extorted by that country's National Civil Police (PNC), which was believed to be even more corrupt than Mexican authorities.

Gabriela, an 18-year-old woman from Honduras, told her story of being tricked into accepting work at a local brothel.

"I was told that I would be working as a waitress in *Tapachula* when I came here at the age of 16," she said, "but the restaurant turned out to be a bar. I was made to *fichar* (a term used to describe spending time with bar customers and boosting drink orders). This *fichar*, often led to a private session with the customer in the back room, which I did not want, but it was the only way I could afford to repay the owner for room and board. It was like being a slave. I was trapped.[36] Finally, I made the decision to leave — to travel to Mexico City by bus, but the authorities stopped the bus and found me without documents. I had no money to pay them, so they brought me here. I have been here for three months and I still don't know when they will release me!"

"We can only trust in God!" Abigail declared.

"Yes, that is my prayer, that God will surround me with his guardian angles," Gabriela replied.

One after the other, their stories confirmed the same grim truth. At least 80% of women who had attempted to travel north through Mexico had been raped. Women and girls, especially those traveling alone and without papers, were at greatest risk. If they were discovered traveling in remote areas or by train, they were likely to be raped.

Many of the border gangs referred to this kind of sexual violence, *cuerpomátic* (using one's body for credit), as a form of currency that could be substituted for monetary payment as a bribe or to buy *protection*.[37] The likelihood of rape was so high that smugglers often recommended that young women get a contraceptive injection before beginning their journey.[38]

Araceli, a 22-year-old Guatemalan, hobbled over on her crutches to join the discussion.

"I was raped the first day I got to *La Arrocrea*. I had traveled there to catch *La Beastia* (the train known as *the beast*)," she stated matter-of-factly. "I was trying to get to Los Angeles, where I have a brother. I was raped by men from the gang *Barrio 18*. They told me that it was my fee for being allowed to ride on the roof of *their* train. After two nights riding on the roof, I was knocked off by a tree branch while I slept. As you can see, I fell under the wheels and it cut off my leg. I hope to get help at the *Jesus el Buen Pastor* shelter in *Tapachula* when I am released."

The infamous freight train, "The Beast", also known as *tren de la muerte* (Train of Death), begins its run departing every 8-10 days from the town of *Arriaga*, about 150 miles from *Tapachula*, then heads northward on to central Mexico and eventually to the U.S. border. For some unknown reason, it is not closely monitored by border authorities, so it is used extensively as a transport option for undocumented immigrants seeking to travel north.

Migrants crossing the border at *Tapachula* who wish to ride the train, have either a dangerous two week walk to *Arriaga*, or they must rely on taking *combis* (taxis) between the eleven immigration checkpoints—exiting each taxi before the checkpoint, walking through the rough brush country around it—board another taxi once past it—leave before the next checkpoint, and so on.

In skirting through the remote bush country around checkpoints, the migrants become vulnerable to one of the notorious Central American gangs that operate all along the train lines. These gangs, *Barrio 18*, and *Mara Salvatrucha*, working in cooperation with corrupt Mexican officials, freely prey on the migrants with little challenge by police or military. These savage gangs also control the train car rooftops and demand bribes from anyone desiring to ride. Those who don't comply are either abused, robbed, raped, or later pushed from the rooftops when the train is moving.[39]

The highly tattooed gang hoodlums, who call themselves "migrant hunters," also lie in wait to rob migrants when they hop off the slow-moving train to avoid upcoming checkpoints.

Riders who are successful in securing a spot on the rooftops cling there—desperately exposed for hundreds of miles, trying to avoid fatal falls and low-clearance tunnels, while suffering through Mexico's hot days and frigid nights.

Even train operators themselves are suspected of collusion with the gangs. Riders report that the train sometimes makes mysterious, unscheduled stops in remote areas of the route, allowing gang members to board, who then rob the passengers.

After hearing Araceli's story of her experience on the train, Abigail exclaimed, "How horrible! What about the bus? Why not take busses instead of the train?"

"Taking the bus can be almost as dangerous—the same gangs rob and assault people outside of the checkpoints, and with the bus you have to get off before every checkpoint, walk for miles to get around each one, and then look for another bus on the other side. Getting on, getting off, and trying not to draw too much attention—the bus drivers know who is illegal and often charge five times the normal fare. One driver told me that he has had passengers robbed on his bus at least one time per week by criminals who boarded as passengers."

"Don't the criminals worry about being caught by the checkpoint police and military authorities?" Abi asked Araceli.

"No, they are corrupt as well—bribed by the criminals, and are often even working with them," Araceli shrugged. "I have heard that first-class busses are waved through checkpoints without an immigration check, but that is not guaranteed and first-class is very expensive!"

In her discussions with the women, Abigail had learned a great deal of useful information, but she still had no clear idea of how the family should proceed on their journey through Mexico after their release. There appeared to be no means of travel, other than flying, that was without great risk.

It was Abi's tenth day of detention, and still there had been no word on the DNA results or on the status of her husband.

For the most part, conditions at the facility had been decent. The women and children had access to water and were fed three meals a day—which was adequate, but there was very little variety, and sometimes the food was spoiled. The women could purchase hygiene items, snack food, and telephone cards at a small store—if they had money.[40] Due to the overcrowding all the beds were filled when Abi arrived, but she and Saul had recently moved from sleeping on the floor to a bunk when some women were released.

During the day, the women had access to an enclosed patio area outdoors, but at night they were locked inside the sleeping quarters.

Many of the women complained of harsh or overly-aggressive treatment from the staff members. The language barrier seemed to be partly responsible for the disrespectful comments and occasional physical mistreatment inflicted by staff members on non-Spanish speaking women, who often did not understand or were slow to obey an order. Abigail was grateful that her command of Spanish had allowed her to avoid that problem.

She was at the bathroom sink, washing out a change of underwear for Saul, when her name was called over the intercom. She was being summoned to the attendant's station outside the main dorm room. She and Saul had a visitor, she was told.

Abi was ecstatic! This visitor must be Samuel—he had been released, so the family should all be together soon. She gathered up her son and was taken down the hallway to a small visitor's room that was furnished with three grey metal tables, each table flanked by two metal chairs.

The attendant told her to be seated, informed her of the 20-minute time limit, and signaled through the window for her visitor to be escorted inside. Abi took a seat on one of the metal chairs, pulled another over for Saul, and the two sat anxiously waiting for Samuel.

Moments later the family was reunited—at least for 20 minutes. After the family's emotional hugs, kisses, and tears of joy, Samuel began to discuss their situation.

"Abi, they issued me a 30-day transit visa, so we need to be out of Mexico in a month. We must get you and Saul released quickly, so we can go. Will the DNA results be back soon?" Samuel asked.

"They have told me nothing, Samuel. I ask them every day, but they just tell me, "They'll come when they come!" I am beginning my ninth month of pregnancy Samuel, I cannot give birth here in Mexico—I cannot—not in a jail," she pleaded!

"Abi, we need to have faith. Please do not lose hope—God will rescue us!

Every day Samuel returned to visit his family hoping to hear that the DNA results had arrived.

Every day Abigail cried out to her jailers, asking them to release her, and every day she cried out to God.

"God, it is just me and my son here—separated from my husband, and we are alone. We have no one in this country to help us. God, I am about to give birth—I am already having pain. Please God, rescue us from this dark place!"

Samuel was becoming frantic. If his 30-day visa were to expire before Abigail was released, he would have to return to jail and start the process all over again—and in 30 days, the baby was due!

Following his release, Samuel had found a room at a *Tapachula* hotel. The Palafox hotel was located in the center of the city and had become a popular refuge, catering to African immigrants who, like Samuel, had recently been released from detention—and the hotel even offered exit visas on credit. The hotel's front steps had become a common gathering place for migrants from Eritrea, Somalia, Ghana, Ethiopia, and elsewhere to visit and exchange stories while listening to music on their cell phones. As a bonus, hotel guests were typically ignored by both police and local gangs.

Many of the migrant guests, now with transit visas, would hang around the hotel for days or across the street at an internet café, waiting for money transfers to arrive from family members back home.[41] They then hoped to take long-haul busses, or fly if they had the money, to northern Mexico where they would ask for asylum at the U.S. border. Those who had been robbed or had run out of money would have to attempt the trip, either riding the gang-controlled train rooftops, or risk playing "Russian roulette" with the gangs and corrupt authorities who terrorized the short-haul bus lines.

Samuel felt fortunate—he had just enough money stashed away to fly his family to the border. But they would need to go soon, because the $11 cost per night to stay in the hotel was quickly depleting their savings.

Chapter 16

Race to the Border

Twenty days had passed, and still no DNA results. Samuel had decided that he could no longer afford to stay in the hotel, but a sympathetic manager permitted him to sleep nights outside on the concrete slab of the hotel's courtyard. He was eating only an occasional bag of chips each day or, on rare occasions, a sandwich— just enough to keep him going for just a few days more—he hoped.

As always, he visited Abi and Saul each day but did not tell them that he was sleeping outdoors on the ground and was going without adequate food, for fear of further upsetting his wife.

Abigail had been experiencing a great deal of pain, and she was fearful that the baby might come early. She had persuaded the dorm attendant to leave the door unlocked at night so that she could sleep on the floor in the hallway outside—and closer to staff personnel in the event of an emergency.

It was the morning of January 19th. Abigail and her son had now been in detention for 40 days. Samuel's travel visa would expire tomorrow when he would be required to return to jail and start the whole process again. Abi's pain was increasing in both frequency and intensity, and she had come to the awful realization that her baby would, likely, be born inside a Mexican jail.

She heard the familiar voice on the dorm intercom. *Morning instructions, as usual*, she thought, but this morning would **not** be as usual.

"Abigail Okotie-Eboh from Angola—Abigail Okotie-Eboh of Angola. Come to the attendants' office; **you are being released!**" The DNA results had finally confirmed that Saul was, indeed, her son!

Abigail fell to her knees. With her face on the floor, she gave praise to God, "Praise you most heavenly father! Thank you Jesus!" She sobbed. "You have rescued my family after 40 days like Jesus in the desert—like the 40 years to cross over into the Promised Land!

Abi used her calling card to contact Samuel and tell him the amazing news. She and Saul had finally been released and now, also, had their coveted transit visas.

After gathering their few belongings, she and Saul stepped outside to freedom for the first time in nearly six weeks. Samuel had hired a taxi and was on his way to pick up his family.

Soon, Samuel's taxi pulled up outside the detention center's entrance. With the possibility that the baby could come at any moment, there was no time to waste!

After a quick embrace, he hurried the family into the back seat of the yellow and white Nissan, and they set off to Tapachula's International Airport, less than 10 miles away.

Samuel studied the flight schedule for the two major carriers, AeroMexico and Volaris, and found a Volaris flight that would take them, with only one stop in Mexico City, to the U.S. border at Tijuana, Mexico. It was due to depart in just over an hour.

He stepped up to the counter and requested three one-way tickets for that flight. The attendant had just begun to process the tickets and examine the family's travel documents when she glanced over the counter and was alarmed to see Abigail's, unmistakably, pregnant condition.

"Oh sir, your wife is so pregnant! The airlines cannot allow anyone more than 28 weeks-along to fly without a medical certificate. I am certain that she is far too pregnant to get a medical clearance. I am so very sorry!"

The couple was stunned. They had not even considered that there might be a flying restriction. *What would they do now? What other options did they have?*

Devastated at the news, Abigail and Samuel crumpled onto seats in the waiting area to recover their senses and ponder their next move.

"Abi, we will have to go by bus. It is the only way now!" Samuel offered reluctantly.

"The bus will take too long, Samuel, it takes at least four days—the baby might come."

"It is the only way," Samuel insisted, "or we will have to stay here until the baby comes and then go through the visa process all over again."

"You and Saul go ahead of me—you can go on the plane and I will come after the baby.

"Abi, there is no way that we would go without you! Whatever we do, we will do it together just like we have always done!"

Now resigned that there was no other option, Abigail declared, "OK, then we will go on the bus. We will pray to God that the baby waits!"

30 minutes later they were at the *Terminal de Autobuses* near the center of *Tapachula*. Of the two major long-haul carriers, ADO offered the lowest fares. The bus line operated three tiers of service, from their Premier luxury level, down to their 1st and 2nd class service.

Samuel was discouraged to learn that the next scheduled ADO departure would be several hours away, and even then, it would be very expensive. However, there was a lower tier option on an obscure "*Holiday*" bus line that would depart within the hour—and the fare would be only $100 each.

Samuel bought tickets for the next scheduled *Holiday* departure, grateful that the less costly bus fare would leave them a small reserve of money for the remainder of the journey.

The economical bus line offered northbound service departing six times per day, so the family had only a short wait and was able to depart at noon.

Holiday's busses were much less plush than those of the major lines, but the couple was grateful for the option and were happy to, finally, be on their way.

The final destination city, *before crossing the U.S. border at San Diego*, was to be San Diego's neighboring city, *Tijuana*, Mexico. The travel distance from *Tapachula* to *Tijuana* was over 2,000 miles and would require four non-stop days of travel with bus stops in major cities along the route, including *San Christóbal de las Casas, Mexico City, and Guadalajara*. The remaining route would take them up the eastern side of *the Gulf of California* to *Hermosillo* and finally west along the U.S. Mexican border to *Tijuana*.

Abigail settled into her seat, lay her head back against the headrest, and took several long deep breaths—allowing herself to consider for the first time in months, that together they had survived this challenging ordeal and were actually beginning the final leg of their journey.

She tried to ignore the frequent waves of pain and to keep herself as calm as possible, believing that undue anxiety about the baby would only hasten the birth.

Samuel had distracted Saul with a game of "I See Something," and the boy was excitedly scanning the view outside the window to find an object that would fool his father.

Economy busses like those of *Holiday* bus lines were known by the locals as a *Tijuaneros*. For many Mexicans and particularly Central Americans, the *Tijuanero* was one of few direct transportation options for people who wished to travel north. Cut rate busses like these were often in *marginal* operating condition. This bus did have a functioning bathroom, but the air-conditioning delivered barely-cool air at best.

Abigail's seat-reclining mechanism was broken, so Samuel switched seats with her. Even the minimal amount of recline helped to reduce the pressure on her stomach.

The bus droned on uneventfully for two hours toward *San Christóbal de las Casas* before it was stopped at the first military check point.

Highway check points such as this one were operated by agencies including the state police, the federal police, the INM (National Migration Institute), and the Mexican army. Only the INM had the legal right to request and inspect immigration documents, but **all** official agencies were known to intimidate and extract bribes from frightened travelers.

The bus came to a stop and the door was opened by the driver. Two soldiers dressed in standard Mexican Army camouflage fatigues and bloused boots approached and one stepped up into the bus.

"*Todo el mundo del autobus* (everyone off the bus)!" ordered the soldier.

Abi woke Saul who had been sleeping across his father's lap, and the three family members followed the other passengers off the bus. The soldiers separated the passengers in two lines, one for women and one for men. Saul was allowed to stay with his mother, as were the other small children.

The Army check point amounted to little more than a tent by the side of the road and a table where three more soldiers sat, looking completely bored.

One by one, each passenger's documents were checked. Any irregularity found on a document or a passenger's nervous demeanor would result in a barrage of questions and, in some cases, harassment from the soldiers.

As each passenger was cleared, they were allowed to return to the bus. Samuel and Abi's transit permits were found to be in order, so they were allowed back onto the bus along with their son.

Of the entire busload, one woman and a young man had been held back—both seemingly engaged in animated conversations with the soldiers. The man was observed taking something from his back pocket and handing it to the soldier, then he was promptly released and allowed to board the bus. However, the unfortunate woman was escorted into the soldier's tent. The bus driver was then ordered to drive on with no explanation offered by the soldiers as to the fate of the female passenger.

The bus's passengers were made up of a diverse group of people. Most were Mexican citizens from *Tapachula's* home state of *Chiapas*, with others coming from Central America—El Salvador, Guatemala, Honduras, and Nicaragua. Other than Samuel and his family, none of the others appeared to be African.

Undoubtedly, many passengers carried questionable or falsified documents, but only time would tell how they would fare with the gauntlet of authorities yet to be encountered as the trip went on.

The bus continued north, traveling day and night and stopping only briefly to drop off or pick up passengers, take on diesel fuel, make a meal stop, or for the daily change of drivers. Occasionally, along local routes the bus would be boarded by vendors who would ride along for a few miles to sell their sandwiches, snacks, or tacos.

On day two of the trip the poorly functioning air-conditioner stopped cooling altogether, so the interior temperature had become oppressively hot and humid. Over the trip, the bus would be passing through six of Mexico's seven climate change zones and, so far, every zone had been uncomfortable.

The frequency of checkpoints and the intensity of the scrutiny increased as the bus neared the U.S. border. By day three, Samuel had counted more than a dozen stops. No matter what the hour, day or night, the routine at each checkpoint was always the same—exit the bus, line up and present documents to some official, be thoroughly hassled, and if you were traveling with questionable papers—pay a bribe in order to be released. The process never differed—only the uniform and locations changed.

Now, in addition to the other inspections, Federal police were actually boarding the bus to search for drugs or other illegal contraband.

There had already been some attrition of the ridership, as several passengers had been detained at earlier checkpoint stops, and this possibility was creating a growing anxiety among the passengers.

Abigail had been in pain day and night for all three days of the trip, and their little boy was well past his threshold, having been confined for so long in the hot cramped space.

As exhausted and uncomfortable as the ride had been, they were thankful to be riding the 2,000 miles on the bus rather than on the roof of *la beastie*.

It was the fourth day of travel, and the bus had just passed through the city of *Hermosillo*. From here they would be crossing the scorching *Sonoran* desert but, thankfully, the nighttime passage should spare them the worst of the heat.

Four hours later the bus was scheduled to have reached *Nogales* on the Mexican side of the U.S. border, but instead sat on the side of the road with a flat rear tire—still 50 miles south of the city.

Samuel, along with several other men, volunteered to help the driver put on a spare, but so far they had been unable to remove the outside wheel which had to be removed in order to access the deflated inner tire of the dual wheel assembly. For two hours, the men struggled, twisting and hammering with hand tools, but the huge wheel lugs would not budge. Unfortunately, it would require a pneumatic torque wrench to loosen the nuts.

Finally, with no help in sight, the driver decided to drive on with only one of the dual wheels inflated. The bus crawled along at an excruciatingly-slow speed for the remainder of the trip into *Nogales*. There the passengers would wait at a truck stop while the tire was repaired and reinstalled.

Since the truck stop was located close to the city's downtown area, the driver suggested that the passengers take some time and explore the blocks of bars, strip clubs, hotels, and restaurants that catered to the mostly U.S. tourist clientele.

The couple had no interest in visiting this sleazy area of the city, but now, only blocks away from the U.S. border, they were tempted to end their journey here at the

Arizona port of entry rather than at the Tijuana / San Diego crossing—another eight-hours bus ride to the west.

Although one would expect the legalities and treatment of immigrants to be consistent among all U.S. ports of entry, Samuel had heard reports that the U.S. authorities at the Nogales border were much less sympathetic in their treatment of asylum seekers than those at the San Diego entry port. Even though the family was exhausted and Abigail was suffering relentless pain, they decided it best to continue the trip, as planned, to Tijuana.

An hour later they returned to the bus for the last push, now into a fifth day—on to Tijuana.

For hours at a time, Abigail lay in the aisle, attempting to reduce the stress on her abdomen and relieve her pain.

Samuel, beside himself with worry, knelt down beside her.

"Abigail, tell me what is going on—how can I help you?"

"I'm OK Samuel, I will be alright. God is with me!"

For most of the trip0 Samuel had been unable to sleep, consumed with worry that if something should happen to Abigail out here on the road and far from any medical help, that he was powerless to do anything for his wife or unborn child.

He knew that what he *could* do, was to pray.

"God, I am trusting you to give us grace so that we can reach our destination. Please God, protect my wife and children. I can do nothing but have faith in your goodness. Amen."

Chapter 17

Welcome to America

Only half the seats were still occupied by the time that *bus* 242 pulled into *Central de Autobuses de Tijuana*. It was 9:45 p.m. on the 24th of January, and the trip had taken nearly five full days rather than the scheduled four, due to the flat tire and extensive repair time in *Nogales*.

The weary travelers gathered their belongings and filed off the bus into the brightly illuminated terminal. Mexico was home to the largest bus network in the world, and this terminal, which served the combined *Tijuana*/San Diego population of six million people, was understandably busy.

Even though the hour was late, the couple had planned to walk from the terminal to the U.S. border crossing about one mile away, but with the increasing possibility that the baby would come soon, Samuel signaled for one of the yellow taxis which were queued along the curb outside.

In a few short minutes, the taxi had reached "Pedwest," the newly constructed pedestrian facility that served the busy *San Ysidro* border crossing. This crossing, the busiest land border crossing in the western hemisphere, processed pedestrian traffic of up to 24,000 people per day in addition to the typical 70,000 vehicles which drove across.

The cab pulled over on *Via Oriente* and the family climbed out. Samuel led Abi and Saul up the steel and concrete ramp which would take them over the 14 lanes of red tail lights, heading north below. They merged into the stream of northbound pedestrians and began to walk across the elevated walkway that spanned between the two nations.

The couple's emotions alternated between disbelief and elation as they approached the actual border marker. Abigail gazed in admiration at the tall, beige concrete monolith that had the words "United States" displayed in bold, three-dimensional letters and the greeting "Welcome" written below. She hoped that the country was actually sincere in that overture.

It was almost too much to take in now that the family was within sight of the "Promised Land." *Were they now, after all that the family had endured, only steps away from this refuge of hope and security?*

As the mass of pedestrian traffic inched its way forward, the corridor was split into three pedestrian lanes, the *Sentri* only lane, dedicated to trusted travelers who had been extensively pre-checked and had purchased a sentry pass, a *Ready* lane, for those holding pre-approved documents, and a lane designated *general public*. At this time of night, only the lane serving the general public was busy.

After 20 minutes in line, the family approached one of the eight open U.S. immigration kiosks. After declaring their African citizenship and presenting their documents, Samuel stated their request, "My family is requesting temporary asylum in the United States. As Christians, we have fled from the killing and persecution by Boko Haram in our home country. We plan to travel on to the safety of Toronto, Canada where my wife has family. Canada is our final destination."

The Immigration officer time-stamped their documents and began to outline the process that would begin with their formal request of asylum.

First they would have an initial screening by the CBP (U.S. Customs and Border Protection agency), then they would be turned over to U.S. Immigration and Customs (ICE). ICE would make the determination whether the family should be detained or released while their case was reviewed by the Department of Homeland Security and immigration courts. And then, even if asylum were granted, the entire process would be quite lengthy.

The family had undoubtedly come from an area of extreme violence but, even so, they wouldn't necessarily qualify for asylum. An asylum seeker also needed *valid* documentation and first-hand testimony to prove a *well-founded fear* of persecution due to race, nationality, or religion. Those who were unsuccessful could very well face deportation; all of that remained to be determined.

Saul normally had little to say. The little boy had become accustomed to long waits and uncertainty over the past several months, but now spoke up, asking his mother, "Mommy, are we home now? Will this place be our home?"

Abigail caressed her son and answered, "Baby, we are safe now in America, but I don't think it will be our home. We will finally be home when we get to Auntie's house in Canada. Then we can have a life!"

The family was escorted to another room where they waited for two more hours to be interviewed by CBP officers. The interview was intended to confirm their basic claims, but it did not involve in-depth scrutiny. After a half hour of questioning, the officer had made his determination. The family would be placed in detention until they could be cleared by Homeland Security. They did not have sufficient corroborating documentation to warrant their release at this time, so their final judgement would have to be made by an immigration judge.

The couple had hoped that Immigration might be more lenient, but they were not surprised by the decision. The family would be split up again—for a while, but praise God! This was America! Here they would be safe and fairly treated!

For the third time in three months, but hopefully the final time, Samuel and Abigail were separated—with Saul again being placed with his mother.

Before being transported to their respective gender designated dorms, digitally coded wrist bands were affixed to the wrists of all three family members, and the two adults were issued standard ICE orange jumpsuits and flip-flops.

The *Otay Mesa Detention Center* was constructed to house a maximum capacity of 1040 detainees but, like detention centers in neighboring countries and in Europe, it was currently operating beyond capacity.

The gray concrete facility had the look and feel of a prison. The perimeter was surrounded by a twelve ft. tall chain-link fence which was topped by rolls of razor wire. Inside, the detainees were held in *pods*, large rooms furnished with bunk beds for 100 people. Here the inmates would eat, sleep, and be confined for up to 23 hours a day, with only one hour to exercise outside.

The variety of nationalities represented among the detainee population was similar to those the couple had experienced before, with asylum seekers from Mexico, Cuba, Haiti, Ethiopia, Somalia, Honduras, Colombia, El Salvador, and Iraq.

After having conversations with other inmates, Samuel was beginning to fear that their treatment here in the U.S.

might not be any better than what they had endured in Nicaragua or Mexico.

Even though each of them had proven a "credible fear" of persecution—the required first step to gaining asylum— many inmates had been in custody for three months and many as long as six.

Several had received inadequate medical care with some being denied treatment altogether. And others had been waiting months to receive any care at all.

Samuel was particularly worried about Abigail. She was now in continuous pain and needed to be examined right away. He could only pray that she would receive proper medical attention.

It had been three long days since the family had been placed in detention. In the women's facility, Abigail and Saul had received meals but for whatever reason had not been allowed to shower or bathe.

Abigail's pain had increased to the point that she was now crying out to the guards, pleading to be taken to a hospital.

"Please—iiiiyaaa! The pain is so severe. The baby is coming—I know that the baby is coming! Please let me go to a hospital—please!" The female guard, seemingly unconcerned, replied, "Your pains are too far apart. We will send you when it is *time* to send you."

This scenario went on continuously throughout the next two days. Finally, at 2 a.m. on the morning of the 29th, the guards decided to send the pregnant woman, who was now in *sufficient agony*, to Sharp Chula Vista Medical Center, a hospital, 20-minute drive north of the detention facility.

Chapter 18

Abigail's Angels

Monica, the delivery nurse on duty, had listened to Abigail tell her story and was in tears. She approached the bedside and gently squeezed Abigail's hand. "Abigail, whether or not the baby comes tonight or tomorrow—I will not allow the hospital to send you back to jail. Somehow I will find a way to keep you and your babies here!"

"Oh Monica! You are my angel. God sent you to be my angel." The grateful woman whimpered.

Within an hour, the doctor had examined Abigail and found that he would need to perform an emergency "C-section"— the baby was in distress.

Abigail was frightened, both for herself and the unborn baby. She had no idea how to notify Samuel and knew that she would be alone for this delivery but was comforted that her new angel, Monica, would be with her during the surgery.

Before she was wheeled into the O.R., Monica prayed with Abi, asking God for a successful delivery and to give her strength and peace throughout the procedure.

Abigail was given a spinal block to numb her from the chest down, as she would remain conscious for the surgical delivery. The C-section procedure had become a common surgery here, as in most delivery rooms across the world, so the delivery team was anticipating nothing unusual with this one.

In moments the baby had been pulled from Abi's abdomen. She had felt some sensation of tugging but no pain. While an intern began stitching her incision to close the wound, the delivery doctor and the attending staff were huddled around the crying infant and conversing in hushed voices. Abi sensed that something might be wrong with the baby.

Monica came closer to Abi, bending over the new mother and gently stroking her hair, she said, "Abi, you have given birth to a beautiful little boy. He is having some trouble breathing, so he will be taken to get an MRI. As soon as the doctors can determine the problem, he will go to the NICU (Natal Intensive Care Unit), and then we can let you see him.

And Abi, I am very sorry—we believe that the baby has *Down syndrome*."

"Monica, I don't know. What is this—this Down syndrome?"

"It is a condition caused by a defect in one of the baby's chromosomes. The disorder can vary in severity but often it causes some intellectual disability and developmental delays, and it can cause other health problems. The baby's blood will be tested to give us more information. Abigail, I am so sorry!"

"Monica, I will love this baby—no matter. I don't care! We prayed for God to give us this baby and he answered our prayers. He blessed us with THIS baby. I will love him and take care of him. This baby will be able to do whatever God wants him to do."

Samuel had been moved to another facility of the *Otay Mesa* complex and had no idea what was happening with his wife and son.

It was lunch time in the men's prison, and the inmates had just been called to have their lunch outside in the barbed-wire enclosed yard.

Samuel did not feel like eating lunch, as his stomach was upset with worry. Today he would stay alone inside the common room and pray for his family.

Falling to his knees on the floor in anguish, he cried out, "Father God, I know that you hear my prayers because you have protected my family and brought us this far. Please hear me again today as I ask you to be with

Abigail and my children, and God—please, please, rescue us from this prison!"

Before the other men had returned from lunch, Samuel heard his name being called over the loudspeaker—"Samuel Okotie-Eboh, report to the guard station."

Samuel rose from the floor and walked to the thick glass-enclosed control station which looked out over the large common room. *What could they want with him now—is there another problem?* he asked himself.

"Are you Samuel Okotie-Eboh?" the guard inquired. "Let me see your wristband."

Dutifully, Samuel held up the band for the guard to scan—still wondering why his name had been called.

"You are being released," the guard stated flatly. "Your wife has delivered a baby, and your little boy has no one to care for him, so you are being released. You can go to the hospital."

Samuel was stunned. *How could this be? God was so good! God had surely answered his prayer and rescued them again!*

Samuel was more than happy to return the orange prison jumpsuit and change into his own clothes, worn and dirty as they had become. With his release papers in hand and the total of his life possessions stuffed into his scruffy khaki-colored backpack, he set out to find the hospital. There was very little money left of the travel fund—less than $50, so the facility's receptionist was kind enough to call an Uber rideshare car to keep his trip cost as inexpensive as possible.

The hospital was located only 12 miles from the detention center, so Samuel was picked up by the Uber driver and dropped off at the hospital in less than 30 minutes.

Abigail was unaware that her husband had been released, so it was a wonderful surprise when he walked into the room.

Saul, the first to see him shouted, "Daddy, Daddy, you came!" The little boy rushed to his father, hugging him tightly and burying his head in his father's thigh.

Abigail, not believing her eyes, threw her arms open wide and sobbed, "Samuel—my husband, God has brought me my husband!"

The three embraced—kissing and sobbing with joy for several minutes until Samuel exclaimed, "Abi, they told me that we have a baby boy! I will name him Gabriel. His name means "God is our strength!" My baby's name is Gabriel. Where is my son Gabriel?"

"Our baby is in intensive care Samuel. He was born with a condition called Down syndrome. It could affect his development and cause other health issues. He is also having some breathing problems, both with eating and breathing. I don't know how long he will need to stay here."

Samuel went immediately to see his boy in NICU and found the infant asleep inside a temperature controlled, glass enclosure. The baby had a breathing tube inserted into his mouth and was receiving oxygen assistance from a nearby machine.

Samuel reached in to caress the tiny body. "Gabriel. I named you Gabriel even before you were born. It means, "God is our strength! You are beautiful—perfect to me—and you are made in the image of God! When you want to talk, you will talk. When you want to walk, you will walk. You will be able to do anything that God has for you to do, and I will be your father. You are my boy, Gabriel."

Later that evening the doctor came in to give the couple more information regarding the baby's condition, taking considerable time to explain the cause and effects of Down syndrome and the list of complications that could develop as the child grew older. He also described the infant's breathing problem in further detail.

The baby was born with a constricted trachea. The opening was smaller than normal, which restricted the baby's ability to inhale air into the lungs or expel it easily. The same condition made it difficult for the child to feed.

Gabriel would need to stay in the NICU for at least a week and then, possibly, have surgery to increase the opening of the trachea.

When the doctor had completed his explanation, Samuel seemed unaffected. He looked straight at the doctor and declared, "Doctor, my baby is fine—he is good—my boy will be OK. We prayed, asking God to give us a baby, and this is the baby he gave us. We praise God for him!"

The doctor, appearing somewhat puzzled, stood to shake Samuel's hand and simply replied, "all right then," as he turned and quietly left the room.

For the next three days as Abigail healed from the surgery, Saul and Samuel slept in the cramped room with her. They had no money left and no place to go, so they had no other option.

Sympathetic hospital staff members, led by Abi's angel Monica, had done everything they could do to make the family comfortable. By this time, much of the hospital staff had heard of the family's story or had personally interacted with the inspiring couple. The couple's remarkable faith, their boundless joy and amazing gratitude—even in these challenging circumstances, was an inspiration to all who encountered them.

Generous hospital employees, and people from Monica's church who had heard about the family's plight, had donated enough money to cover their immediate needs for food, bus fare, and incidental items, and had donated clothing items for all three as well.

The doctors had determined to keep Gabriel hospitalized for another week but were ready to release Abigail. The family still had no place to go.

Monica had attempted to find a source of help for the family, but so far she had not found a place for them. She had also recruited her friend Linda, the hospital's social services coordinator, to see what she could do through her social service agency contacts.

The family would be put out onto the street by the end of the day and Abigail, who had no means of transportation, would need to somehow get to the hospital every day to deliver breast milk for the baby.

Just before the family was about to be ushered out of the hospital, Monica received a call from Linda. At the last moment, Linda had secured a motel room for the family, and it was close to the hospital—but only for one week, no more.

"Wow, God has given us another miracle," Samuel sighed with relief.

The next week passed with the baby's condition still too serious for him to be released. Linda had continued to scour her social service resources, attempting to find a shelter that would take the family in for a few more days. She found a shelter that would accept Abi and the three-year-old but would not allow males over 15 years of age to stay at the facility. Samuel would have nowhere to go. He would have to sleep on the street.

Abigail was racked with despair when she heard the news. Again, she called out to God, "God you brought Moses and his people out of Egypt and into the promised land; Moses struck the rock and you gave the people water. It is me, Abigail—now praying for you to give me a miracle. God save us from this. My husband cannot be put out on the street again!"

"Linda, I will go onto the street and stay with my husband. I cannot be sleeping in a warm bed while he has to sleep on the street!"

Linda pleaded, "Abigail, it is all we can do at this time. You must go to the shelter—at least for your son, Saul. He must have a safe place to sleep."

"Samuel, I haven't given up yet! I'm still trying to find you a place, even though it won't be with your family."

It was amazing, God had to be at work here! Again, when there seemed to be no hope, Linda received a phone call telling her that a bed had "unexpectedly" opened up in a men's shelter that was located about five miles from where Abi and Saul would be staying. Even though Samuel would need to take the bus and make several connections to see his family, he would at least have a safe place to stay.

Abigail and Saul were dropped off at the women's shelter that evening and assigned beds and issued bedding. The shelter's director was quite pleasant but also business-like. The woman was obviously a person of compassion, but she had heard every sad life story that a woman could tell and had little interest in hearing Abigail's.

"You are welcome here between the hours of 6 p.m. to 6 a.m. You will be awakened at 5:30 every morning, and you must vacate the building with all your belongings by 6 a.m. No exceptions!" stated the director.

"You mean that we can't be here *at all* during the day and we must take all our belongings with us," Abi asked, surprised to hear the strict rule.

"Yes, I'm sorry — no exceptions."

"I don't know where we will go during the day. We can't stay all day at the hospital. My baby is in the N.I.C.U."

"You can go to the city library, but it doesn't open until 9:30 a.m. You would need to take a bus, but they will allow you to sit inside as long as you are quiet," offered the director.

At precisely 5:30 a.m. the next morning, the lights came on in the woman's dorm room along with a recorded announcement reminding guests that they must vacate the premises by 6 a.m. Abigail gently patted Saul's arm to wake him.

"Mommy, I'm too tired—I want to sleep," Saul protested.

"I'm sorry baby—you have to get up now. We have to leave soon, but we can come back later this evening."

Abi hurriedly dressed herself and then helped the little boy into his clothes. After making the bed, she grabbed the handle of the roller bag that Monica had recently given her and followed the other residents out the door.

It was still dark outside, so she was grateful for the shelter's well illuminated perimeter lighting. Even for a moderate climate like San Diego, the early morning air was a cold 49°.

The library would not open for several hours; however, one of the shelter's residents had mentioned a nice park which was a few blocks away, so Abi, with the roller-bag behind and her son beside her, set off to find the park.

The sun was just beginning to rise by the time they reached the park. The park was part of a huge green-space shared with the famous San Diego Zoo and Balboa Park, so it was well maintained and clean. The large expanse of grass and large shade trees were a welcome change from last night's sterile concrete shelter—and even from the cold antiseptic environment of the hospital.

Abi found a bench next to a park restroom and lay Saul down with his head on her lap. Thankfully, the building blocked some of the frigid air coming off the ocean. *This was the best she could do for now*, she thought.

Abi began walking directly to the library each morning, after leaving the shelter. She and Saul would sit on the bench, waiting in the cold outside for the next three-and-a-half hours until the library opened.

Even though he was not required to leave his own shelter at that hour, Samuel would take the bus to meet them at the library every dark cold morning.

Abigail was hardly sleeping and was awake with worry most of the night. The long bus rides to the hospital every day to see Gabriel and deliver breast milk, combined with the stress of nightly separation from Samuel, was taking its toll on her.

This dark morning, as she sat waiting with her son on the concrete bench outside the library, her head dropped to her chest as she nodded off.

"Wake up! You can't sleep here!" the security guard barked, shaking her shoulder.

"I didn't mean to fall sleep. I was just so tired, I was just resting," Abi replied.

"You will have to leave this area if you fall asleep again. It's not allowed by city law."

"I will stay awake sir," Abigail promised.

20 minutes later the guard was back, "You need to leave ma'am. I'm sorry but you can't stay here any longer. You were asleep again."

"Please don't make us go away from here—my husband won't know how to find us. He only knows how to find us here!" Abigail pleaded. "I **will** stay awake! This time I **will** stay awake—if I don't, we will leave."

The security guard looked at the distraught woman and the small boy and felt compassion. "One more chance," he said. "I have to do my job, so **please** stay awake this time."

Abigail now knew what she must do—she would make a joyful noise to the Lord! She pulled herself straight up on the bench and began to pray and sing praise songs. God would help her to stay awake as she lifted up her voice in joyful praise to him.

Chapter 19

Finishing Strong

For weeks, the couple had followed the same routine, up at 5:30 a.m., meet at the library by 6:30, ride three busses to get to the hospital, spend time with their baby, and return to their respective shelters around 7 p.m. It was a grueling time for all, especially for Saul. It wasn't the life that a three-year-old should be living, but they had no choice — this is what they had to do.

Gabriel's condition had improved somewhat, and the doctors were considering releasing him to go home. *What home?* Abigail wondered.

They desperately wanted to go on to her sister's home in Canada, but now, having exhausted their savings, they were entirely beholden to the generosity of social services.

Two weeks later, even though she was still housed in the shelter, baby Gabriel was released to his mother. Abigail was deeply concerned that the fragile infant, having such a weak respiratory system, must now be exposed to the cold mornings outside just as she and Saul had been experiencing.

Abi had recently gained another angel, Gina—another of Monica's friends who had been *touched* by the faith of this amazing family.

Gina took every opportunity to lighten the family's spirits. When she had time off from work, she would take them all out to eat, take Saul to a playground, or just have them hang out with her own family—anything to give them time away from the depressing shelter environment and allow them time to be together.

But just as Abi feared, the baby had become ill and was struggling to breathe—with an audible wheezing, accompanied by the inability to eat. He was rushed back to the hospital and into intensive care.

This time the doctors determined that they would have to perform surgery on the baby. They would attempt to enlarge the opening of his trachea, hoping that the result would improve his ability to breathe and take in food.

Abi prayed for God to protect her baby in this surgery and to provide a way for them to *finally* reach Canada, their final destination.

Again—she prayed and God answered!

Linda was on the phone with amazing news. She had found a place for the entire family to stay—**together**! She had secured an apartment in Chula Vista that had cooking facilities and beds for the entire family—for a full 60 days!

This was unbelievable—this never happened. Even Linda was in disbelief!

The apartment in Chula Vista was such an amazing blessing! This was the first time that the family had really all been together since leaving the hotel in Costa Rica three months before.

For almost two weeks, while Gabriel recovered from the surgery, Abigail spent days and nights there with him at the hospital. Samuel cared for Saul at the apartment at night and then, every day, the two made a series of bus connections and a three-hour-ride in order to travel 18 miles to the hospital—followed by the same long bus ride home each night.

As soon as the baby was well enough to leave intensive care, Abi moved back to the apartment. The family continued to make the exhausting bus trip to visit baby Gabriel each day until he was finally strong enough to come home.

Meanwhile, Monica, her team of angels, and the family's new friends from church, had been gathering donations to pay for the family's airfare to Buffalo, New York, just across the border from Abigail's sister in Toronto, Canada.

Linda, utilizing her social service contacts, had located a family shelter in Buffalo that had agreed to accept the family upon their arrival there. From Buffalo, the family's final hurdle to a new life would be Canadian immigration.

Even though the family now had adequate documentation, California I.D., and Canadian relatives who were anxious to take them in, their chances of being granted entry were not guaranteed.

Finally with the baby's condition stabilized, the family was scheduled to leave for Buffalo—leaving in three short days to complete their long journey.

Before they left, Monica's church asked the couple to participate in a videotaped interview in order to document the incredible story of their three-month journey—knowing that the story of their remarkable faith and their trust in God's goodness would have continuing impact.

These powerful comments, taken from the end of their interview, pick up after Monica and Linda had secured the apartment for the family.

Interviewer

Abigail, can you tell us how it felt to have a place where the family could finally be together again and be somewhat settled after such a long struggle?

Abigail

That day Monica and Linda came to fetch us, to pick up our things to take us to the apartment. I said, Monica, Linda, I don't have anything to give you. I don't have diamonds or gold. For what you guys did for me you deserve something in return—may God bless you and your families—may God give you long life that you can see your grannies and great grannies and the gift of eternal life. And that is all I have to give you. Thank you very much!

Linda asked us—maybe we can do something to help you. Maybe some fund raising, maybe some posting on Facebook?

Linda, I said, any way that God touches your heart to help us. I don't need to be spoon fed—I can work for myself but right now I am in a new country with a sick baby, please, if there is **any** way that you can help us to get to Buffalo—to Canada—my sister. She wants so much for us to be with her. She has no children of her own. She adopted her husband's children. She wishes to see me with the children. That is how they say they will help us!

So that is how Monica and Linda started making all the arrangements for our traveling and such things.

Samuel

God used them to help us — God used them to rescue us—in our situation. We give all thanks to God!

Abigail

Yesterday, Monica told me, "Do you know that people in the church raised some money for you guys to help you get to Buffalo?" And what you guys did for us yesterday, it's so not what I expected *(Monica had arranged for a special dinner, with all their new friends and supporters, to honor the family and to celebrate their victory of traveling on to Canada)* I grew up with the idea that people in the United States, they are racist—they don't like black people and I, with my family, in the hand of white people? Me with my black skin welcomed by white people? God fearing? I did not know that there were God fearing white people. I thought that maybe white people thought of themselves as Gods.

I came to this country—I didn't have anything. I didn't have clothes, only one pant and one dress. My husband only have one pant. This boy—we lost everything when the woman who was helping us was arrested. She was carrying everything for him.

So my son, every day in the hospital, people bring clothes for him, stuff for us. **God is wonderful. I don't know how to thank this God!**

Samuel
I'm telling you, we have a lot of clothes. We have a lot of things. We have so much that we cannot take it all to Canada!

Abigail
All I want is for God to use me! I want my dream—I have now, this disabled child—I want to help disabled children and the mothers through my faith. Let me

change the lives of others, let me work for them, let me offer my community service. I'm not expecting anything in return. I just want to work for God!

Interviewer

What is one thing that you have learned on this journey that you would like for other people to know?

Samuel

God has taught me that first there must be **faith.** The second is to be **united**—when you are united, you can move the mountain. We, I and my family, we are united all the way from Africa to here and you have to be **praying** because God answers prayer!

Abigail

And to me—I can say that what my husband said—it is **faith.** Through this journey, God increased my faith so much! God helped me so much. God used **people** to help so much. God teach me how to have unlimited love for another person and God teach me not to neglect another person—no matter how the person look like, what color is the person, what age is the person. You don't know tomorrow, who will help you. You understand?
Because of that, the **love** I meet in the United States, I wish if I had a place to stay my husband was working, that we could stay in the United States. For the love I found and the faith I found in the United States people. God gave this

country, not just to Americans—it is for all people! **I say God bless America!**
I talk to my friends on Facebook. I tell them what I went through—they don't believe! God opened the road for me. I came to this country—no visa—illegally, how I get here. Nobody believe how I get here!

Samuel

Come from **far**—walking, running, through the mountain, on horse, and I reach the United States, and found people that were God fearing, that have strong faith and welcome us. Wow!
God said, "**Go**, I have my people to help you along the way!"

Abigail

And my last word is—I want to thank the pastor and all the church people that welcome us. Monica took our family to the church. I will always love you guys and keep you in my prayers. Just keep doing the good work. I will pray for all of you to live a long life and to be in paradise with us—joyful and praising God! Thank you for all the love you show my family. May God bless you all abundantly! Amen.
Samuel
And **God bless America!**
Abigail

And **God bless America!** This country will always be blessed— that is why, when I look at the dollar, the one dollar—it says "In God do we will trust,"—the same God that I trust—and the same God that the members of this church trust—so please, keep going in that trust!

Saturday, April 23rd

The family made it successfully through San Diego Airport security, to catch their flight to Buffalo. They were approaching the finish of this incredible journey.

May 6th at 8:33 pm

This, anxiously awaited, text was received by all of the family's new friends:

"Dear friends, I just wanted to let you know that our amazing family just crossed the border into Canada. **Praise God**, and thank you for your amazing support. My heart is full"—love Abigail

God had delivered Abigail and Samuel out of the darkness—out of "the shadow of death." Because of their amazing faithfulness, they had been brought into the light!

Who among you fears the LORD
    and obeys the word of his servant?
Let the one who walks in the dark,

**who has no light,
trust in the name of the** LORD
and rely on their God. Isaiah 50:10 NIV

Epilogue

Meeting this family and hearing their incredible story impacted my life in ways that I am still processing. I may never fully appreciate the scope of their influence in my life.

There is no doubt that their story and their personal examples provided real life illustrations of what *true* faith looks like. I'm not sure if I will ever muster up that level of faith in my own life.

It is one thing to talk about "having faith" and "trusting in God." Allusions to those fundamentals are almost habitually included in our everyday spiritual dialogue — but demonstrating those beliefs *"when the rubber hits the road"* in real life circumstances is another thing altogether. I have witnessed through this couple's example that demonstrating true faith *is* possible.

Wouldn't it be amazing if, as a country, we demonstrated the attitudes that Abigail and Samuel experienced, *the treating of aliens with kindness and unlimited love?* I am afraid that often we do not.

Wouldn't it be wonderful if Americans truly lived by the slogan printed on our currency, *"In God We Trust?"* I am afraid that for the most part, our citizens do not.

One of Abigail's statements—actually more of a declaration—was that *"America, so enormously and undeniably blessed by God, did not belong only to us, but to everyone!"*

My selfish nature wants to disagree with that idea, after all, I am a citizen of this country. I was born here—as was my father, and his father, and so on — I belong. I own property. God provided these gifts to me and my family. It is easy to forget that at one time, all of our families were immigrants.

We can't just open the American floodgates to all the needy and less fortunate of the world. *Can we? Where would that leave us? Where would that leave our children?* And besides, even Jesus remarked that the *poor* will always be with us.

I believe that God has responded to the past generosity of our country by blessing us beyond any other. Over its short history, America has accepted more immigrants than any other country in the world, with the current number being close to 85 million, if birthright citizens are included, a full 25% of our total population.

Our country, like many throughout the world, is dealing with horrible acts of violence and discord among its citizens, as well as threats from outside our borders. We are weighing tough political solutions and are considering extreme actions in the hopes of restoring a sense of safety and security to our lives. We are proposing the *"building of longer, stronger, higher walls," and banning people, "unlike ourselves," from our country altogether.*

As we consider efforts to protect our land, our borders, our way of life, and our possessions, it is interesting to contrast the concept of **legal** ownership with that of **Biblical** ownership in regards to this question.

Our law defines ownership like this: Owner of property: *The owner is he who* **has dominion** *of a thing real or personal, corporeal or incorporeal,* **which he has a right to enjoy and to do with it as he pleases,** *even to spoil or destroy it, as far as the law permits, unless he be prevented by some agreement or covenant which restrains his right.*

In regards to **having dominion**, does that then justify that *"might makes right?"*

My worldly attitude and perhaps yours, is to believe that *everything that I have I worked for! No one gave me anything —I worked hard for it!*

The Bible describes ownership like this:

You may say to yourself, "My power and the strength of my hands have produced this wealth for me." But **remember the LORD your God, for it is he who gives you the ability to produce wealth,** *and so confirms his covenant, which he swore to your forefathers, as it is today.*

(*Deuteronomy 8: 17-18*)

For who makes you different from anyone else? What do you have that you did not receive? And if you did receive it, why do you boast as though you did not?

(*1 Corinthians 4:7*)

Everything belongs to him. (*Colossians 1:16*).

To the LORD your God belong the heavens, even the highest heavens, the earth and everything in it. (*Deuteronomy 10:14*)

"The silver is mine and the gold is mine," declares the LORD Almighty. (*Haggai 2:8*)

Conversely, one can find verses in the Bible that cite *personal* ownership but, of course, this is underwritten by the understanding that all things were created by God, for God, and ultimately belong to God.

I think that in the end our views will be defined by whether we view the things that we have in America as "hard-earned possessions and deserved rights" or as *extraordinary blessings* from God.

If we acknowledge them as gifts from God then perhaps, this scripture should be considered:

"From everyone who has been given much, much will be demanded; and from the one who has been entrusted with much, much more will be asked." Luke 12:48

So what do we do with these ideas? I don't claim to have the answer, but I believe that those of us who are Christians should be mindful of God's direction on these matters, allowing those principals to influence our personal actions as well as our votes.

Our world news consistently reports examples of the international migration crises that are occurring all around the globe. We have, likely, become numb to the problem because we hear these accounts so frequently.

Hundreds or even thousands of African migrants and refugees, not equipped with life jackets, drowned when their flimsy, unseaworthy boats sunk or were capsized in failed attempts to cross the Mediterranean Sea from Africa to Italy.

More than 900 men, women, and children died in the same manner while attempting to cross the dangerous water from Turkey to Greece. By the first part of 2016, over 37,000 migrants had made this crossing to either Italy or Greece, a tenfold increase over the prior year.

Similar scenes have unfolded with migrants from the countries of Myanmar and Bangladesh, enduring brutal, sometimes fatal, conditions to be smuggled in cargo ships across the Bay of Bengal and the Andaman Sea to Indonesia or Malaysia.

Millions of people like these are on the move all across the globe, driven from their home countries by the same factors: political instability, religious or ethnic persecution, war, violence, hunger, economic strife, corruption, and lack of personal opportunity. They are willing to leave everything and everyone they have known, risking brutal hardships and even death, in a desperate attempt to find refuge, safety, security, freedom, and opportunity.

This report from the United Nations High Commissioner for Refugees (UNHCR), also known as the UN Refugee Agency, illustrates the true magnitude of this world crisis:

GENEVA, June 2015 (UNHCR) – Wars and persecution have driven more people from their homes than at any time since UNHCR records began, according to a new report released today by the UN Refugee Agency.

The report, entitled *Global Trends*, noted that on average 24 people were forced to flee each minute in 2015, four times more than a decade earlier, when six people fled every 60 seconds.

The detailed study, which tracks forced displacement worldwide based on data from governments, partner agencies and UNHCR's own reporting, found a total **65.3 million people were displaced** at the end of 2015, compared to 59.5 million just 12 months earlier.

At sea, a frightening number of refugees and migrants are dying each year. On land, people fleeing war are finding their way blocked by closed borders. Closing borders does not solve the problem.

It is the first time in the organization's history that the threshold of 60 million has been crossed.

"More people are being displaced by war and persecution, and that's worrying in itself, but the factors that endanger refugees are multiplying too," said UN High Commissioner for Refugees Filippo Grandi.

Grandi said that politics was also standing in the way of those seeking asylum in some countries.

"The willingness of nations to work together not just for refugees but for the collective human interest is what's being tested today, and it's this spirit of unity that badly needs to prevail," he declared.

The report found that, measured against the world's population of 7.4 billion people, one in every 113 people globally is now either an asylum-seeker, internally displaced, or a refugee – putting them at a level of risk for which UNHCR knows no precedent.

To put it in perspective, the tally is greater than the population of the United Kingdom, or of Canada, Australia, and New Zealand combined. It is made up of 3.2 million people in industrialized countries who, at the end of 2015, were awaiting decisions on asylum, the largest total UNHCR has ever recorded.

Also in the tally are a record 40.8 million people who had been forced to flee their homes but were within the confines of their own countries, another record for the UN Refugee Agency. And there are 21.3 million refugees.

Forced displacement has been on the rise since at least the mid-1990s in most regions, but over the past five years the rate has increased.

The reasons are threefold:

- Conflicts that cause large refugee outflows, like Somalia and Afghanistan, now in their third and fourth decade respectively, are lasting longer;
- Dramatic new or reignited conflicts and situations of insecurity are occurring more frequently. While today's largest conflict is Syria, wars have broken out in the past five years in South Sudan, Yemen, Burundi, Ukraine and Central African Republic, while thousands more people have fled raging gang and other violence in Central America;
- The rate at which solutions are being found for refugees and internally displaced people has been on a falling trend since the end of the Cold War, leaving a growing number in limbo.[42]

For us, here in America, the impact is felt primarily along our southern border shared with Mexico.

The *"Migrant Trail,"* the route which runs through the entirety of Central America and Mexico to the U.S. border, is currently the world's largest migration corridor. The border running from Texas, through New Mexico, Arizona, and to California, was historically the primary entry point used by Mexicans; however, it is now used equally by migrants coming from Honduras, El Salvador, Guatemala, Cuba, Africa China, India, and Pakistan, and many other countries.

As I sit here today, comfortably located in my Chula Vista home only eight miles from our shared border with Tijuana, Mexico, I read this article published in the San Diego Union Tribune newspaper entitled "Cross-Border Response Needed for Refugee Crisis."

The authors, Pat Murphy, a Catholic priest who is the director of *Casa del Migrante-Centro Scalabrini*, a faith based nonprofit shelter in Tijuana, and Peter Gyves, a Catholic priest who founded the interfaith coalition, *Faith That Does Justice*, describe, in their words, *"the beginning of what could be the greatest tragedy in recent years."*

The authors focus on the recent dramatic increase of refugees seeking asylum through the *San Ysidro* and *Otay Mesa* border crossings, just south of San Diego.

Father Murphy has seen his shelter in Tijuana evolve from primarily serving Mexicans recently deported from the U.S., to taking in an entirely new refugee population—recently opening their doors to 600 people from 19 different countries.

He believes that in the near future thousands more will follow, based on the accounts of those refugees already here. Shelters in Tijuana are already over capacity and few realize the extent of what is happening.

The crisis is likely to be compounded by the recent U.S. Supreme Court ruling that could send up to 4 million deferred deportees (undocumented people, mostly Mexicans, who have U.S. born children and families with no criminal record) back to Mexico.

Another huge factor is the economic depression being experienced by South Americans.

More than 150 Haitians recently applied for asylum here after migrating first to Brazil, only to experience the deepest recession in recent memory in their adopted country. They then traversed the dangerous route through Panama, Costa Rica, Nicaragua, and finally Mexico, in their efforts to reach the U.S.

On the Mexican side of the border there has also been a stark rise in homeless—destitute families spending days and nights on the street while waiting to be processed by U.S. authorities. They are so fearful of losing their place in line that they remain there near the crossing, with no food, blankets, or money.

The reality is that, even though they are legally entitled to an asylum hearing, very few will be granted access.

Most will be turned away due to insufficient documentation of their claims of threats or violence.

Father Murphy's article ends with this plea, "We need people willing to *be the voice for those that have no voice* in order to make others aware of the crisis at our border.[43]

Looking back full circle to Nigeria where our story with Samuel began, conditions have not improved.

This statement is from "The San Diego Union Tribune," Thursday August 4, 2016—

The new leader of Boko Haram, Abu Musab al-Barnawi's first public statement was to declare his focus of "bombing churches and killing Christians."

Describing the Christian threat, he says, "They strongly seek to Christianize the society. They exploit the condition of those who are displaced under the raging war, providing them with food and shelter, and then Christianizing their children."

al-Barnawi promised to respond to the threat by "booby-trapping and blowing up every church that can be reached, and killing all of those (Christians) who we find from the citizens of the cross."

And in Somali, Al-Shabaab, a Somali group that the United States designated as a foreign terrorist organization in March 2008, wants to turn Somalia into a fundamentalist Islamic state, according to the Council on Foreign Relations.

In 2011 a U.S. official, who declined to be identified because of the sensitivity of the information, said the group was estimated to control up to 1,000 fighters.
A United Nations report identified one insurgent leader alone who is believed to command an estimated force of between 200 and 500 fighters, most of them Kenyans.[44]

Al-Shabaab's spectacular and deadly attacks killed 74 football fans watching the 2010 World Cup final in a pub in Kampala, Uganda, and shoppers on a sunny 2013 Saturday morning in Nairobi, where 72 died at the Westgate Centre.

Inside Somalia, the country's citizens live under the repressive rule of an organization that banned smoking cigarettes, watching televised sport, listening to music or even wearing a bra, all deemed to be un-Islamic.[45]

In June of 2016, at least 14 people were killed when Al-Shabaab gunmen stormed a hotel in Somalia's capital and took an unknown number of hotel guests hostage. This assault, which began with an explosives-laden vehicle blowing up at the hotel gate, lasted for hours.

While these and countless other horrific reports provide examples of a world in chaos, we are privileged to live in America, the greatest, most blessed, and safest nation on Earth.

I must admit that if faced with similar conditions of violence and persecution that exist in many other nations, I would likely, legally or illegally, uproot my family and join the migration exodus.

As you and I formulate our individual positions on immigration and its long-term implications for our country, it may be worthwhile to keep in mind the famous quote from John Bradford, **"There, but for the grace of God, go I"**.

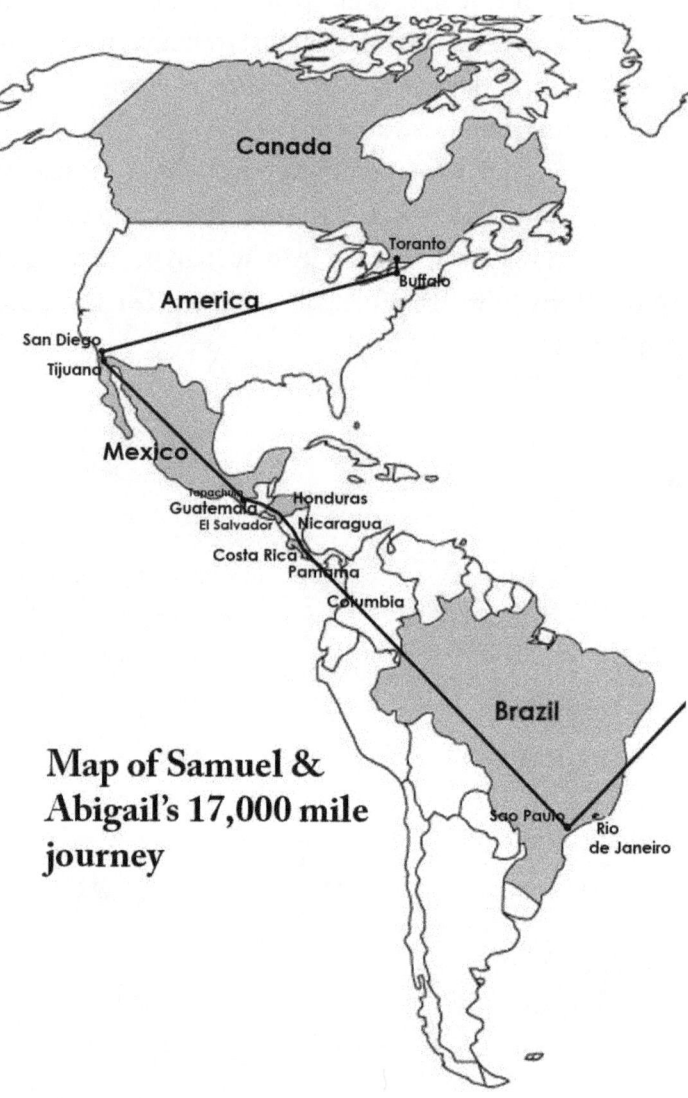

Map of Samuel & Abigail's 17,000 mile journey

Run From The Shadow   231

Photo Gallery

Terminus Market (before bombing) Page 21
Courtesy of Travel Advisor-Nigeria

Boko Haram bombings Jos, Nigeria Page 21

Courtesy of https://www.flickr.com/photos/diariocriticove/14237725034

Sao Paulo Favela Courtesy of Anthony Goto   Page 53
https://www.flickr.com/photos/anthony_goto/2322604135

Melanito Biyouha at Biyou' Z   Page 58
Courtesy of Lufe Gomes http://www.eatinerario.com/en/home/biyouz-restaurante-africano-centro-sao-paulo/

Run From The Shadow 235

Biyou' Z   Page 57
Courtesy of http://www.nikkeyshimbun.jp/2014/140614-gourmet-biyou-z.html

Carnival Samba Dancer at Sambadrome   Page 61
Courtesy of Mauricio Roja, CC BY-SA 3.0, https://commons.wikimedia.org/w/index.php?curid=35505327

Run From The Shadow 236

Chicken Bus *Ruteado*   Page 131
Courtesy of
Barry Pousman https://www.flickr.com/photos/castle_life/5782322870

Darian Gap Jungle   Page 94
Courtesy of
https://www.flickr.com/photos/everypassingminute/311 215590

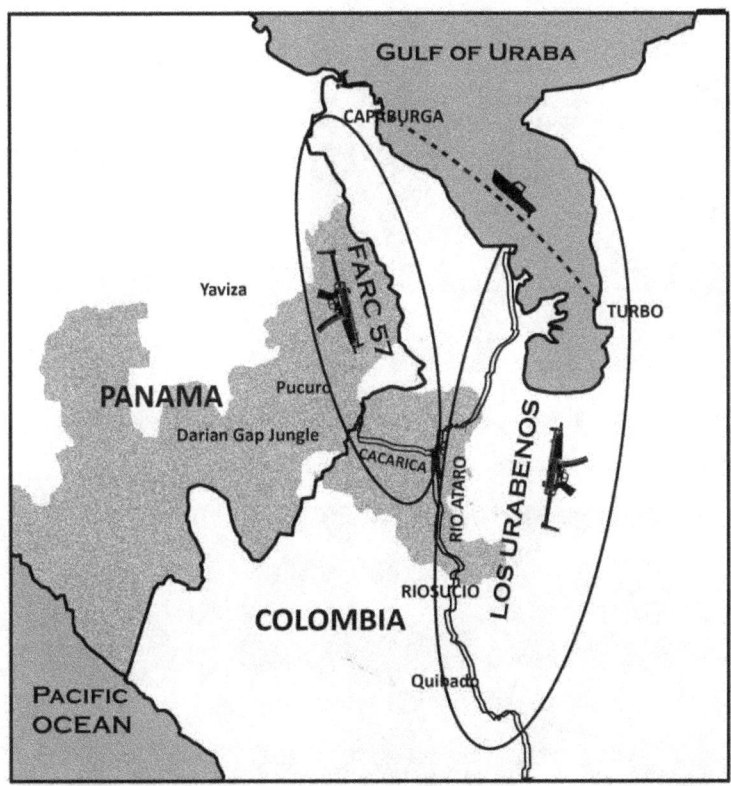

Map of Darian Gap Jungle/ Panama/ Colombia

Howler Monkey   Page 111
Courtesy of Angela, N. https://www.flickr.com/photos/aon/4677025594

Horseback over Nicaraguan border   Page 144
Courtesy of J.P.Maithani https://voices-and-visions.com/2013/06/22/

Run From The Shadow 239

Police Patrol Nicaragua Pages 112-116
Courtesy of jorgemejia Foter.com CC -https://aulablog.net/category/Nicaragua

Río Atulapa Courtesy of CC0 Public Domain Page 152
https://pixabay.com/en/river-rocky-forest-outdoor-nature-1031551/

Run From The Shadow

Guatemalan Police Truck — Page 154
Courtesy of RudyGironphotos.rudygiron.com/stock
https://www.flickr.com/photos/antiguadailyphoto/5754052474

Guatemalan Policeman — Page 155
Courtesy of Bill Meech
https://www.flickr.com/photos/billhmjr/4703580004

Run From The Shadow

Suchiate River crossing · Page 159

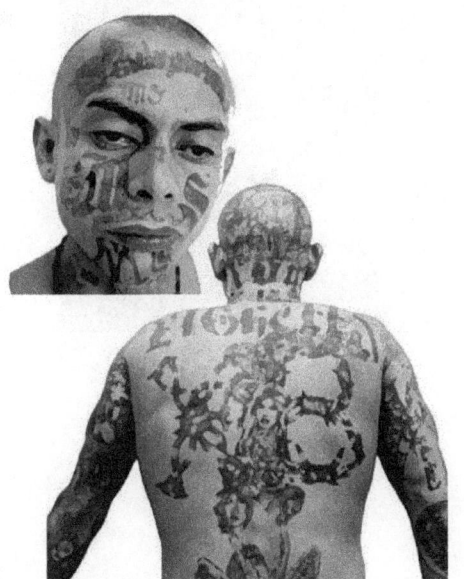

Mara Salvatrucha (MS-13) Gang · Pages 155, 169
(Typical full body tattoos)

Riding "The Beast Page 168
Courtesy of FORECASTS & TRENDS E-LETTER

Riding "The Beast Page 168
Courtesy of FORECASTS & TRENDS E-LETTER
by Gary D. Halbert August 14, 2014

ACKNOWLEDGEMENTS

For 40 years, my amazing wife, Karen, has had my back in every, foolish and not so foolish, endeavor, that I have attempted.

Her unconditional support has allowed me to experience wonderful successes, and her nonjudgmental love, has allowed me grace in failure.

The writing of this book was no different. Karen has never questioned the goal, or questioned my ability to prevail, instead, she has provided positive support and enthusiastic affirmation of my efforts, every step of the way.

Thank you Karen, for your love and support — even through the hours and months of selfish, single-focused writing.

Thank you, also, to my son Grant, my beautiful daughter-in-law, Kelly, my mother, Dixie, and my sister, Sharon, for your prayers, ideas, support, and encouragement.

Special thanks to Monica, Linda, and all of Abigail's angels.

References

1 *The unexplored territory of Nigeria's Used Spare Parts Market.* (2015, July 10). Retrieved May 15, 2016, from http://africabusiness.com/2015/07/10/the-unexplored-territory-of-nigerias-used-spare-parts-market/.

2 Ibid

3 *2014 Gamboru Ngala attack.* (2014, December 23). Retrieved from Wikipedia: https://en.wikipedia.org/wiki/2014_Gamboru_Ngala_attack

4 Adoyo, Sarah. (2014, May 20). *Between 118 And 200 Killed, Scores Injured In Jos Twin Bomb Blast.* Retrieved from NAIJ.com: https://www.naij.com/66705.html

5 *Rampant growth spells trouble.* (2008, May 30). Retrieved from Fin24 Archives: http://www.fin24.com/Economy/Rampant-growth-spells-trouble-20080530

6 *Angola Rising Cultural Traditions: The Bride Price.* (2011, February 15). Retrieved from Angola Rising.com: http://angolarising.blogspot.com/2011/02/cultural-traditions-bride-price.html

7 Thomas von der Osten-Sacken, T. U. (2007, Winter). *Is Female Genital Mutilation an Islamic Problem?* Retrieved from Middle East Forum: http://www.meforum.org/1629/is-female-genital-mutilation-an-islamic-problem

8 *Marriage in Islam.* (2014, April 23). Retrieved from Wikipedia.com: https://en.wikipedia.org/w/index.php?title=Wali_mujbir&redirect=no

9 Ibid

10 Ibid

11 *Background.* (2016, April 15). Retrieved from Human Rights Watch:
https://www.hrw.org/reports/2003/angola0803/5.htm
12 Dolan, K. A. (2013, September 2). *Daddy's Girl: How An African 'Princess' Banked $3 Billion In A Country Living On $2 A Day.* Retrieved from Forbes.com:
http://www.forbes.com/sites/kerryadolan/2013/08/14/how-isabel-dos-santos-took-the-short-route-to-become-africas-richest-woman/#33f82c5d79fe
13 *Angola country summary.* (2011, January). Retrieved from HRW.org:
https://www.hrw.org/sites/default/files/related_material/angola_0.pdf
14 Allen, Michael . (2010, June 19). *The 'Blood Diamond' Resurfaces.* Retrieved from wsj.com:
http://www.wsj.com/articles/SB10001424052748704198004575311282588959188
15 Kristof, Nicholas Op-Ed Columnist. (2015, March 19). *Deadliest Country for Kids.* Retrieved from nytimes.com:
http://www.nytimes.com/2015/03/19/opinion/nicholas-kristof-deadliest-country-for-kids.html?_r=0

16 *Sao Paulo: Population and Slum Housing - GEOCASES.* (2016, May 15). Retrieved from geocases 1.co.uk:
www.geocases1.co.uk/printable/Housing%20in%20Sao%20Paulo.htm
17 Swartz, B. (2015, April 27). *Sao Paulo Culinary Backstreets.* Retrieved from culinarybackstreets.com:
http://culinarybackstreets.com/cities-category/elsewhere/sao-paulo/2015/biyouz/
18 *Afro-Brazilians.* (2016, July 27). Retrieved from wikipedia.org:
https://en.wikipedia.org/wiki/Afro-Brazilians

19 History of Carnival Retrieved from Rio.com:
    http://www.rio.com/rio-carnival/history-carnival
20 *Sao Paulo Carnaval*. (2016, July 27). Retrieved from carnival.com:
    http://www.carnaval.com/brazil/saopaulo/carnaval/
21 *Crime in Brazil*. (2016, July 27). Retrieved from wikipedia.com:
    https://en.wikipedia.org/wiki/Crime_in_Brazil
22 Addley, E. (2016, March 17). *Why is Brazil's government in crisis? – the Guardian briefing*. Retrieved from theguardian.com:
    https://www.theguardian.com/world/2016/mar/17/brazil-government-crisis-briefing-dilma-rousseff-lula-petrobas
23 Biller, D. C. (2015, April 21). *Drought, Dengue Fever Is Now Sweeping Across Sao Paulo*. Retrieved from bloomberg.com:
    http://www.bloomberg.com/news/articles/2015-04-22/after-record-drought-dengue-fever-is-now-sweeping-across-sao-paulo

24 Romero, S. (2015, December 30). *Alarm Spreads in Brazil Over a Virus and a Surge in Malformed Infants*. Retrieved from nytimes.com:
    http://www.nytimes.com/2015/12/31/world/americas/alarm-spreads-in-brazil-over-a-virus-and-a-surge-in-malformed-infants.html?_r=0
25 Cowie, S. (2015, September 2). *Sao Paulo massacre highlights disturbing trend in Brazil*. Retrieved from aljazeera.com:
    http://www.aljazeera.com/indepth/features/2015/09/sao-paulo-massacre-highlights-disturbing-trend-brazil-150901091245319.html
26 Guy, D. I. (2015, August 15). *18 killed in city's deadliest massacre this year*. Retrieved from guyana.hoop.la:
    http://guyana.hoop.la/topic/18-killed-in-city-s-deadliest-massacre-this-year-1
27 Goodman, G. (2016, July 27). *How to Ride a Nicaraguan Chicken Bus*. Retrieved from adventuresofagoodman.com:

http://www.adventuresofagoodman.com/how-to-ride-a-nicaraguan-chicken-bus/

28 Connell, D. (2016, Spring). *Eritrean Refugees' Trek Through the Americas*. Retrieved from merip.org: Ghebre and this is my friend Tesfay

29 Conexiones, N. (2015, February 6). *What It Is Like In The Immigration Detention Center, Managua, Nicaragua*. Retrieved from http://nicaconexiones.com/what-it-is-like-in-the-immigration-detention-center-managua-nicaragua/

30 Salisbury, L. (2015, September 28). *Top 8 Unusual Sights in Managua, Nicaragua*. Retrieved from http://somethinginherramblings.com/: http://somethinginherramblings.com/top-8-unusual-sights-in-managua-nicaragua/

31 Goodman, G. (2016, July 27). *How to Ride a Nicaraguan Chicken Bus*. Retrieved from adventuresofagoodman.com: http://www.adventuresofagoodman.com/how-to-ride-a-nicaraguan-chicken-bus/

32 *MS-13*. (2016, July 27). Retrieved from wikipedia.org: https://en.wikipedia.org/wiki/MS-13

33 McDonnell, P. (1991, January 8). *Guatemalan Town Is Dangerous Stop on the Road North*. Retrieved from articles.latimes.com: http://articles.latimes.com/1991-01-08/news/wr-7928_1_tecun-uman

34 *Living in Liminality, Welcome to The Jungle Border*. (n.d.). Retrieved from anphilabaum.wordpress.com: https://ianphilabaum.wordpress.com/2014/07/11/el-paso-de-los-coyotes/

35 Bacelar, A. (2016, April). *In Photos: The Central American Migrant's Journey to Asylum*. Retrieved from emersoncollective.com:

http://www.emersoncollective.com/articles/2016/4/28/in-photos-the-central-american-migrants-journey-to-asylum

36 Grayson, G. W. (2002, July). *Mexico's Forgotten Southern Border: Does Mexico practice at home what it preaches abroad.* Retrieved from cis.org: http://cis.org/MexicoSouthernBorder-Policy

37 McIntyre, E. S. (2014, October 9). *http://fusion.net/*. Retrieved from Is rape the price to pay for migrant women chasing the American Dream?: http://fusion.net/story/17321/is-rape-the-price-to-pay-for-migrant-women-chasing-the-american-dream/

38 Ibid

39 Isacson, A. M. (2014, June). *Mexico's Other Border.* Retrieved from wola.org: http://www.wola.org/files/mxgt/report/

40 Diaz, G. G. (2008, June 2). *Women Migrants in Detention in Mexico: Conditions and Due Process.* Retrieved from migrationpolicy.org: http://www.migrationpolicy.org/article/women-migrants-detention-mexico-conditions-and-due-process

41 Fox, C. (2016, January 8). *More African and Asian Migrants Are Arriving in Mexico After Long Latin American Journeys.* Retrieved from news.vice.com: https://news.vice.com/article/more-african-and-asian-migrants-are-arriving-in-mexico-after-long-latin-american-journeys

42 Edwards, A. (2016, June 20). *Global forced displacement hits record high.* Retrieved from unhcr.com: http://www.unhcr.org/en-us/org/en-us/

43 Murphy, P., & Gyves, P. (2016, July 29). Cross Border Response Needed For Refugee Crisis. *San Diego Union-Tribune*, P.B7.

44 Yan, H. (2015, April 2). *What is Al-Shabaab, and what does it want?* Retrieved from

http://www.cnn.com/2015/04/02/world/africa/al-shabaab-explainer/

45 Pflanz, M. (2015, April 3). *Al-Shabaab profile: A history of Somalia's insurgent movement* http://www.telegraph.co.uk/news/worldnews/africaandindianocean/somalia/11513886

www.ingramcontent.com/pod-product-compliance
Lightning Source LLC
Chambersburg PA
CBHW031308060426
42444CB00032B/193